MANAGING QUALITY OF SERVICE

By Alan Lawrie

MANAGING QUALITY OF SERVICE

By Alan Lawrie

First published 1992
Revised edition 1995

© 1995 The Directory of Social Change

The Directory of Social Change is a registered charity no. 800517

The Directory of Social Change
24 Stephenson Way London NW1 2DP
Tel: 0171 209 5151
Fax: 0171 209 5049

ISBN 1 873860 86 2

British Library Cataloguing in Publications Data
A catalogue record for this book is available from
the British Library

Designer: Kate Bass

Printed in Britain by Biddles, Guildford.

Alan Lawrie is an independent consultant and trainer who works with public sector and voluntary agencies on management, organisational and strategic development.

Contents

Introduction

The past ten years have seen considerable changes in the way in which organisations have managed their work, with the introduction of new funding arrangements creating a much greater emphasis on measurement and accountability.

Nearly every aspect of public expenditure has come under greater scrutiny. Auditing, inspections and requests for management information have expanded considerably and are now a key part of the political and managerial process. It is no longer enough just to do "something good or worthwhile". Now you have to prove that income allocated is being used in an effective way, that activity does produce worthwhile results and that the project is worthy of further investment.

The issue is not just driven by external pressures and demands. Many organisations have lacked any real information or feedback to help them decide if they are meeting their aims and values. Often organisations lack a sense of progress and achievement. Subsequently there is a lack of any real knowledge about which services and activities deliver sustainable and valued results. Intelligent monitoring systems and processes can help to make informed decisions about future directions and priorities. They can also help to create a feeling of purpose and progress in an organisation.

A critical issue that runs throughout this book is the ability of managers to develop and adapt systems that fit with the identity and often unique circumstances of their organisation. This involves responding to an external demand for measurement and standards in a way that does not see the issue as a threat. Pressure has to be applied to design and negotiate systems that which not only the meet often limited external requirements, but also provide valuable internal feedback.

THE BIGGER PICTURE - THE CONTEXT FOR THIS BOOK

The following seven issues are all part of a background for this book:

1 New systems of control

The past few years have seen the development of much more stringent inspection and monitoring functions. In social care, education and other areas, external inspections and review have been introduced. These inspections are often rigorous and require detailed evidence of good practice and performance.

1 ●

2 The growth of a "contract culture"

The creation of a purchaser and provider divide or client and contractor split whereby one party commissions a service that the other party delivers has had a major impact. A central feature of many contracts and agreements is the requirement that the contractor provides the purchaser with regular information and data on the performance of the contract.

3 A new "management language"

Terms such as "performance indicators", "resource management" and "inputs and outputs" are being used more and more. Much of this language can feel off-putting and get in the way of doing "the real work" but, to continue to provide an effective service we need to understand this language and work within it.

4 A commitment to give users more say

Now there is a much greater emphasis placed on seeking out the views of the people who use a service. Organisations are now expected to demonstrate that they consult with and listen to their users. The introduction of complaints procedures, user feedback forums and advocacy systems all require a much more open management.

5 Public league tables and comparisons

The government's wish is to be able to make comparisons between organisations. In several areas, most notably in schools, hospitals and local government. The government has introduced performance league tables with the intention that people can "choose within a market place of providers". The launch of Citizens Charters is another aspect of this.

6 The rise of quality management systems

Many organisations have invested heavily in quality assurance systems, total quality management programmes and adopted quality standards. Over 28,000 UK organisations have been awarded BS5750. These systems are sometimes criticised for being mechanistic, but are now firmly established in most sectors.

7 The rapid growth of information technology

Most organisation have computer based systems that allow much more efficient collection, collation and presentation of management information.

Several of the management concepts and measurement techniques described in this book were traditionally designed for a commercial or industrial purpose. They have often been imported into arenas such as social care or health with little thought of application or adaptation.

The main purpose of this book is to explain the terms and processes involved. Some of the ideas presented are straightforward, others need translating into a more accessible and useful language and some of the models will require considerable work to make them suit your organisation. They can not be simply "lifted off the shelf". This book aims to unravel these concepts and techniques, identifying those that are genuinely useful and introducing tools and techniques that add value to your work and are a help rather than an extra burden .

THE STRUCTURE OF THE BOOK

Chapter two
> looks at some basic definitions and concepts relevant to this subject and the necessity of having clear aims and agreement about what is important. A simple model of how organisations can be measured is explained and discussed.

Chapter three
> the issue of performance measurement is reviewed. Guidance is given on the use and abuse of performance measures and indicators and a range of possible measures is outlined.

Chapter four
> focuses on the issue of "Value For Money" studies. It looks at what should be included in such a study. It describes the problems involved in trying to use a Value for Money approach to make comparisons between organisations. The idea of added value is introduced.

Chapter five
> the issue of Quality introduced. Different quality management strategies are explained. The critical and difficult issue of defining quality is scrutinised on.

Chapter six
> The different approaches of quality control and quality assurance are considered in chapter six. Practical advice is given on drawing up a quality assurance system.

Chapter seven
> introduces the idea of total quality management.

Chapter eight
> poses questions about the managerial and organisational implications of using both performance measurement and quality systems. How can they change the management process of the organisation? What value does it bring to an organisation?

Chapter nine
> concludes with a bibliography of useful follow up reading.

MEASURING ORGANISATIONS

Broadly speaking there are three ways to look at the effectiveness of an organisation.

1 A Performance model

Collecting information (usually through a system of preset performance measures or indicators) to record what the organisation does over a period of time. Performance measurement should ensure that the organisation is making effective progress towards completing its stated plans or objectives.

2 A Comparative model

Comparing the costs and performance to similar organisations or to possible alternative ways of delivering the same service. Making comparisons is an essential aspect of a "Value For Money" study.

3 Through setting minimum quality standards

A quality assurance approach centres on finding out what are the quality elements that matter to users. These issues are then developed into quality standards. The organisation's systems and processes are then monitored to ensure that the agreed standards are always met.

WHY BOTHER MEASURING?

It is useful to consider why you are spending time looking at measuring performance and quality. Is it because you have chosen to look at how you measure and evaluate your work or is it that other people, (senior management, funders or the people you contract with) are requiring you to do it? Do you have to deal with these issues or have you chosen to?

Which of these factors apply to you?

Internal driven reasons

☐ We want to to know if what we are doing works

☐ We need to evaluate if we are doing the right things

☐ We are committed to high quality work but need to find a way of managing it

☐ We need better information and feedback to make decisions about our work

Externally driven factors

☐ Our funders demand information from us

☐ Resources are tighter. We need to show that we are worth investing in

☐ We have to prove that we provide value for money

☐ We need evidence about the effectiveness of our work

WHY BOTHER MEASURING?

It may well be that you have several reasons for being involved in these issues.

How clearly are the reasons understood and shared throughout the organisation?

....
....
....
....
....

Do people see it as a positive thing or as a threat?

....
....
....
....
....
....
....
....

If your main reasons are external ones you might wish to consider how you take the initiative and make the process useful to you.

....
....
....
....
....

How much control can you have over the process, methods used and focus of the exercise?

....
....
....
....
....

CHAPTER 1

Making Sense Of What You Do

This chapter introduces two sets of questions which need working on before you move into either measuring or setting standards for your work.

The two issues are:
How clear are your aims?
What should the organisation be focused on?

ALL ABOUT AIMS

All organisations have some kind of written aims, goals or objectives. They are called different things by different people. Terms such as objectives, mission, goals and aims are often interchangeable. There is no standard definition, but it is useful to ensure that people in your organisation define their terms and use them consistently.

Sometimes organisational aims are very clear and precise. They give the organisation a united sense of purpose and direction. They act as both an "anchor" that holds the organisation together and as a route map for future direction. On the other hand in some organisations they are vague and lack any real meaning. They were written for legal or constitutional purposes. They have little relationship to what the organisation does. People in such an organisation are sometimes confused as to what it is for and what is important. Surviving from year to year is rarely a good enough reason to keep going!

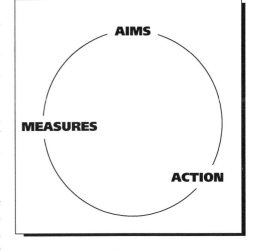

There is a direct relationship between measurement and aims. Good measurement systems need to be directly linked to the aims. The measures used need to be clearly linked to the aims of the organisation or a specific part of it. Good measures can act as milestones that tell you if you are making progress to achieving the aims. They can also provide useful information and feedback to tell you where to next direct your limited resources and effort. They can help to create a feeling that you are achieving something, that the organisation is going somewhere and give it occasional good cause to acknowledge and celebrate your achievements.

HOW CLEAR ARE YOUR AIMS?

Before starting to measure or evaluate your organisation and its work
it is important that you have clear aims to measure against.

1 Is there a written statement
that gives you a clear sense
of purpose and direction?

2 Are your aims clear enough to
help you determine priorities
about where you should
devote resources and time?

3 Do your aims make it clear
who is supposed to benefit
from the organisation?

4 Do they indicate what is
important about how
you should work?

5 Are your aims in such a form
that you can draw from
them specific work plans?

6 Could most people in the
organisation easily explain
what the organisation is for?

7 Can you easily identify
milestones towards
achieving your aims?

MEASUREMENT AS A KEY

The staff group of a regional arts centre held a "think tank" day to review and plan their work. They started with a simple exercise. Participants were asked to identify how they knew if the centre was successful.

In less than twenty minutes over thirty five different possible measures of performance were identified. They included items as diverse as:

- *How much coverage we get in the media.*
- *Attendance levels and waiting lists for classes.*
- *Creation of new local arts projects.*
- *Repeat donations from funders.*
- *Budget balancing at the end of the month/year.*
- *The range of art forms on offer at the centre.*
- *Box office returns.*
- *Repeat visits from schools.*
- *The gender and ethnic mix of people using the centre on a daily basis.*
- *Creation of new and innovative art work.*

The group quickly recognised that different individuals used very different measures. Some were much more concerned about the creative and artistic merit of the centre, others were interested in the centre's use by local communities and there were those whose emphasis was on concerned about the financial and commercial viability of the centre.

The different measures were at the heart of many long running tensions between staff members over the purpose and management of the centre. One person talked about how a lack of measurable progress was often a cause of conflict. Another commented that if they had so much trouble trying to make sense of what was important then what chance would the public and funding bodies have.

A key priority for the centre would be to find a way of measuring the range and different aspects of its work. To do this three questions had to be addressed:

What are we about?
Who is it for?
What is the longer term goal?

**How do we balance the different
elements in our business?**
Popular events versus new innovative work
Work with people interested in art versus work with people new to it
Meeting obligations to funders versus doing what we think is needed

How should we measure our work?
What results are we interested in?
How do we know if the centre is a success?

Measuring without reference to aims can be disastrous. In the absence of any sense of what is important, measures or standards are established for what is easy to measure rather than what is important. Often new people in an organisation are looking for clues as to what is important so that they can establish what they need to do to stay a member of the organisation or even succeed in it. In the absence of clear aims what gets measured is often a strong clue. If the wrong things are being measured than they can easily create a very distorted picture of what is important. Management rhetoric might say that what the organisation values is the quality work and personal time spent with each individual client, but if the measurement systems in use only report on the number of clients seen and how quickly they are processed then an entirely contradictory pressure is being exercised. The requirements of and energy involved in playing the wrong numbers game can very easily produce a very different organisation than what was originally intended.

Good aims are two sided. They indicate what the organisation is for - what it will do and what its strategy will be. They also tell you what the organisation values about how it will do things. What kind of relationship it will have with the people who use it and what are its social priorities. Good aims reflect both the heart and mind of the organisation.

WHAT SHOULD THE ORGANISATION BE FOCUSED ON?

Often managers implement measurement systems without first deciding what are the important things to focus on. Before embarking on any standards setting or measurement exercise it is important that a full view of the organisation is taken. In designing measures and standards it is very easy to only take a narrow view of what you do and only focus on the visible and obvious features. It is easy to design systems to count what is happening. It is usually harder to design systems that measure the effectiveness of what happened.

Much of the practical experience of performance measurement so far is that it often puts greater emphasis on the amount of activity rather than the quality of the results. Volume is measured at the expense of long term effectiveness in meeting or changing needs. A significant distinction that will be looked at later is between being busy and being effective.

For it to work everyone needs to be involved in looking at the bigger picture. We need recognise that some things are harder to measure than others and be prepared to exercise a thoughtful insight into interpretation of findings.

Inputs, Outputs and Outcomes

An established model for measuring performance is one based around identifying and monitoring inputs, outputs and outcomes. Over the past ten years this model has been used extensively in the public sector.

For example, a training agency might be awarded a contract to deliver a training programme to unemployed adults. At the end of the training programme sixteen of the original twenty trainees have successfully completed the course. Three might then go onto college and take more advanced training. Two might have got a job. Others might return to being unemployed.

At its simplest, the main input is the money from the contract and the output is that sixteen students received training. The outcomes are harder to identify but are of real importance. Some of the students went on to further training or work - a clear outcome. Others might not have followed such a route, but still have found the course valuable. For example, one student might have overcome her feelings of isolation, so that in two years time, as soon as her children are older, she will feel much more skilled when she is able to look for work. A valuable outcome, but harder to monitor.

Some points about inputs, outputs and outcomes

We can plan and manage the outputs of a service or activity. How we use and manage the input determines the output. To a greater or lesser extent we are in charge of the design, volume and delivery of the output. The outcomes usually are not always in our direct control. The outcomes are much harder to plan for, predict and therefore measure.

Outcomes are sometimes difficult to objectively prove. It can be difficult to establish that your output was directly responsible for a particular outcome. How can a drugs agency that has made education work with young people a high priority prove that it was its campaign work which was the output that led to a change in behaviour amongst young people?

Outcomes usually take a longer time to develop - the output might have ended (the project has been wound up or moved on to other objectives) without any knowledge of the outcome. It could be that the outcome is a "side effect" of the work.

Every organisation can be described in the following way

INPUTS
↘
    ACTIVITY
      ↘
        OUTPUTS
          ↘
            OUTCOMES

INPUTS are resources allocated or made available for an activity - money, equipment, staff are the most obvious ones.

The ACTIVITY is what the organisation does with the inputs.

The OUTPUTS are the services or activities provided.

The OUTCOMES are the results or effect of the output.

INPUTS, OUTPUTS AND OUTCOMES FOR A COMMUNITY PROJECT

A Neighbourhood Association secured funding to employ a community worker on their estate. The worker produced a work programme for the first six months that had three main aims:

- To support the creation of tenants associations.
- To provide practical help and advice to local people.
- To identify local needs and carry out a fund raising campaign for the neighbourhood association.

The project had the following inputs, outputs and outcomes:

Inputs

The salary of the community worker.
The grant for the project's running costs.
Free office accommodation in the local estate hall.

Other inputs were less obvious:

Volunteer time and effort.
Support and help from local voluntary organisations and local people.

The project outputs included:

- 140 hours work with local people on setting up a tenants association.
- 24 Advice sessions attended by 88 local people.
- Production of a report on the needs of the community.
- 35 hours of work with local parents on a campaign for a school crossing.
- A fundraising campaign with over 150 potential supporters contacted.

The outcomes are harder to objectively record. However looking back at the work, three months later, it was possible to point to the following outcomes:

The tenants association had elected a committee that was now strong enough to meet without the constant support of the community worker.

42 of the people who attended the advice session had had some sort of a positive result.

The report on local needs had been positively received by the Council and there was some hope of more permanent funding.

The fundraising campaign raised £975.

OUTPUTS AND OUTCOMES

Outputs	Outcomes
Usually tangible factors. *What was produced/delivered*	*Changes, benefits, learning* *or prevention*

Training centre

Numbers attending a course	New skills learnt - learning objectives met
Numbers completing the course	Award of qualification/Job success
Feedback reviews about the delivery of the course itself	New opportunities as a result of the course

Local advice service

Number of clients seen	Did advice/advocacy lead to positive gain for client?
Number of hours open	Does client now understand the nature of their problem and is aware of his/her options?
Type/duration of interviews	Did the advice centre improve the economic, social or health profile of the area.?

A campaign to improve home safety

Number of homes visited	Measured decline in home accidents in target group
Number attending talks/classes	Better co-ordination of agencies in the field
Meetings & work with other professionals	Creation of home safety liaison group
Hours/cost of home safety work carried out	Probable saving to taxpayer and family due to prevention

QUESTIONS ABOUT OUTPUTS

Is performance to target?

Is the quantity right and on time?

Is it what was asked for?

Was it worth the input?

What is the instant reaction to it -
do people like it?

Did it meet the specifications?

QUESTIONS ABOUT OUTCOMES

What difference has this made?

What has been the benefit of this activity?

When the activity or output has ended what will
be the lasting benefit?

What have been the side effects of this work?

What will change as a result of this work?

What can we learn as a result of it?

In most situations there are a range of outcomes that could be identified for different people at different times. Some outcomes may be quite quick whereas others take time. The motivational benefits of attending a good training course might be instant, but it will take time for a newly trained individual to put into practice her or his new skills. One approach is to predict different levels of outcomes ranging on a scale from short term (i.e. the immediate impact of the output) to longer term ones that should create sustainable change.

Different people will be interested in different outcomes. For example, in an after school club, the children who attend it will be interested in a lively and exciting programme, their parents might regard a successful outcome of the club to be one which allows them to carry on working and provides good and affordable child care. The school that runs the club might be interested in whether the club supports the educational ethos of the school and is therefore seen as attractive by prospective parents thus leading to an increase in the school's roll.

Measuring outcomes require effort, analysis and interpretation. Despite the difficulties involved in accurately monitoring them, outcomes are usually critically important. They are, in essence, what was achieved (as opposed to what was produced). They should relate back to the original needs that the activity was expected to meet or change.

Often there is a struggle to persuade people to take a longer term view of a service. It is important that managers emphasise that it is the quality and effectiveness of outcome that matters and not only the cost of the input or the quantity of the output.

Several different types of outcomes are possible:

Change based outcomes
Outcomes that meet identified needs or make progress towards them. A community development project could point to several new initiatives that they have helped to create as outcomes of their work that have led to an improvement in the area.

Preventative outcomes
Outcomes that can be shown (or a reasonable assumption made) to stop or prevent a negative progression or likely consequence. A home help service could argue that providing regular support to isolated people in their own homes will prevent the development of more severe problems which could lead to the necessary provision of residential care.

Learning outcomes
Outcomes that test out new ideas or innovations. One national agency ran a development project to try out new ways of working. The level of interest shown in the project was not high and the project struggled to achieve any real success. The output was disappointing, but valuable lessons that could be disseminated to similar projects were identified as a useful outcome.

OUTCOME BASED FUNDING

One recent development is an interest in the idea of funding programmes and measurements systems being directed at outcomes rather than inputs or outputs. Harold Williams and Arthur Webb in their book "Outcome Funding", describe a process of moving away from funding organisations on the basis of the activities they propose to carry out such as "we will run an information service" and instead change the "mindset" of the relationship to creating measurable results.

The key stages in this process are:
- A clear definition of need.
- Agreement of specific targets or results.
- Identification of measurable milestones.
- Measurement of short and long term results.

Some government bodies have started to introduce outcome based programmes, most notably the Department of Health has piloted a series of outcome based funding agreements for drug and alcohol services. Some Training and Enterprise Councils have built into contracts specific outcomes expressed as targets (eg. 75% of students will meet NVQ level 2).

Outcome planning and funding does require radical thinking. Instead of focusing on the funding of the services, the attention shifts to:
- What will be the results of the activity?
- How will the original needs have been met or changed?
- How has this activity made any difference?

Advocates of outcome based programmes would suggest the following benefits:

It is geared to results and change

Programmes must demonstrate that they are able to achieve something that will be sustainable. The organisation has to become more task or result centred. The results should be expressed in qualitative terms such as enabling individuals to learn new skills that enabled them to find and keep a job that they wanted.

It allows flexibility of method

How the service provider meets the outcome is the concern of the service provider and not the funder. A community drugs team working to an intended outcome of helping individuals live a drugs free life might meet this outcome through several different interventions - counselling, practical help around housing and benefits or health related work. The funder should only have an arm's length interest in the detail of how the provider works.

It creates much more useful measurement and planning

Implemented properly it can develop effective measurement, evaluation and planning. Programmes should be able to demonstrate that they do things that work rather than simply how busy they are.

Most of the criticisms of outcome based funding focus on the difficulty and complexity involved in the applying the ideas in practice.

The following points are common criticisms:

Who sets the outcome?

An activity can have many different outcomes for different people. The stated outcomes of a community project working with young offenders could include a reduction in re-offending rates, personal development for the young people, better relationships between agencies working in the field and an anticipated cash saving caused by fewer of the young people re-entering the criminal justice system. But, it is possible to speculate on many other possible outcomes for the local community, individual young people and their families and the police and legal system. The decision to target specific outcomes is a very clear statement of values. Who should make this decision - the funder? the service provider or the user?

It could be open to abuse

One training scheme was issued with a contract which had an outcome that 80% of trainees would receive a vocational qualification. An evaluation of the scheme indicated that a message had filtered down from the scheme managers to trainers only to recruit trainees who were likely to stay the course and get the qualification. The scheme had started "creaming" - picking the people most likely to succeed in order that they would get a good outcome. The contract was very weak on criteria for becoming a trainee so trainees with special needs, access problems or those that would require extra support or help were discouraged or rejected.

It only works if there is a very clear needs assessment

For the intended outcomes to mean anything, time must be spent on identifying the needs and starting points to find out what is a reasonable outcome to set. Often the identification of both individual and group needs is haphazard and is rushed. For outcomes to work there needs to be a clear agreement about exactly from where a programme or intervention is to start.

To operate to an outcome based system requires intelligent thinking, consultation and negotiation as to what is the starting point, milestones and possible outcomes. It requires hard work, radical thinking and collaboration.

CHAPTER 2

Performance Measurement

All of us collect information all of the time to enable us to make sense of things. We carry round in our heads criteria and yardsticks to judge our experiences. We use it to make judgments and decisions - "Today was busier than yesterday" - "x is a good place" - "y often fails to work properly" are all typical of the judgments we make every day. Collecting and making sense of information is a central feature of living, organising and managing.

PERFORMANCE MEASUREMENT DEFINITIONS

Performance

Performance is what gets done and what happens in a specific time. Performance could be what gets produced, gets delivered and is achieved. Some aspects of performance are tangible (eg. the number of training days delivered) other aspects of performance may be less tangible and harder to measure such as a change in behaviour.

Performance measures and performance indicators

Often the terms 'measures' and 'indicators' are used to mean the same thing. There is no strict definition but a common working one is that an indicator is used to record precise information whereas a measure is used to collect less exact information. For example the number of people who stay in a hostel each night is a precise figure that could be recorded through a simple indicator. To record what happens to the people who stayed afterwards would require a more open and more interpretative method to collect useful information.

Performance expectation or performance standard

Standards and expectations are a central part of a quality assurance programme discussed later in this book. Preset standards are agreed and the organisation's performance to them is measured. For example a grant award trust could set a standard to process each application within twenty days. This would become a standard. It would then report on any occasions when it failed to meet its standard.

Performance target

Standards are minimum commitments that we should plan always to keep to. Targets are different. They are policy commitments or pledges to improve performance to a particular level. For example, a community development agency might set itself the target of establishing three projects in the next year. It could then monitor itself against this target.

Profit making companies pay great attention to quarterly and annual results, return on investment ratios, share prices, and the amount of new business on the order book. These measures of performance have been established for many years. The introduction of formal measurement systems in non-profit making bodies is a much more recent development. Over the past ten years, agencies that spend and use public money have been required to develop an often extensive range of measures to report on their performance. Most contracts and service agreements or grant aid arrangements will demand that certain information be collected and recorded on a regular basis.

Performance measurement systems are seen as having the following benefits:

- They provide data by which an organisation can be judged to see if it is working in the way that it said it would and is consistently delivering the intended quantity and quality of service.

- They can tell people what they should be able to expect (e.g. repairs should be carried out within three days). Funders, staff and users can see what kind of service is to be expected and are able to identify failings.

- They provide a focus for managers. A performance measurement system can alert managers to problems or weaknesses and enable them to take action to ensure effective performance.

CASE STUDY

A FEAR OF MEASUREMENT?

The Director of the Hillmore centre expected that the discussion at the staff meeting would be poor, but she still felt disappointed that no progress had been made on the item called "performance and review". The Hillmore centre received European, central and local government funding to run a series of programmes "to benefit the long term unemployed".

At the previous two staff meetings the Director had explained that the centre needed to establish some clear performance measures and standards to provide internal management information and as evidence for funding bodies.

Several of the staff resisted any notion that their work could be measured. The Student Counsellor complained that her work was all about personal development and was impossible to measure. A fear of playing the "numbers game" was expressed. One of the tutors complained that any monitoring exercise would only be about occupancy levels and unit cost and not about the quality of the work.

The Director felt depressed. She would have to produce some monitoring system to keep the funders happy. However, the comments made did hint at a bigger issue:

- If things are so important yet cannot be measured then how do we know that we are doing them at all well?

- If things are impossible to measure how do we know that they are working? Could a reluctance to review the work and measure its effectiveness be hiding something?

- If we do not get feedback then surely we must miss out on a feeling of achievement, results and success.

- They can provide the basis for making comparisons between organisations carrying out the same or similar activity.

- They can help to give an organisation a sense of purpose and to enable staff to recognise achievements over a set time.

- They can provide funders, trustees and policy makers with useful feedback information on how an organisation is doing, what is working and what is not.

- Without information how can you manage or operate with any degree of certainty?

- However in practice many organisations have moved into performance measurement systems (or being dragged into it as a funding requirement) without given much thought to the purpose, process or implications of measuring performance.

Some of the difficulties often met include:

It becomes a "number crunching" exercise

Monitoring becomes a routine chore whereby arbitrarily chosen sets of numbers are collected together and are passed onto an external monitor. They rarely reflect the actual work of the organisation. The performance measurement systems record only what is easy to record rather than what is important.

The systems used do not relate to us

There is a problem of language. The terminology used in performance measurement is often mechanistic, perhaps more suited to accountancy or to a manufacturing enterprise. In fact, one of the first real attempt to develop performance measurement systems was in the Soviet Union in the development of central planning within the command economy - with disastrous results.

Performance measurement systems can rarely deal with anything complex

Trying to express everything in quantitative terms that can be collated and summarised in a brief report ignores the complexity, depth and individuality of what we do.

A FIVE POINT DESIGN GUIDE

1 What is the service or project for?

2 What values should influence it?

3 What do we want to measure?

4 What are the possible indicators?

5 How will the information be used and interpreted?

Many organisations have found the concepts of performance measurement difficult to apply precisely to a field as complex and sometimes intangible as, for example, running an elderly people's day centre. Often this "difficulty" means that performance measurement systems focus on the quantity of the service (eg. how many people used it) rather than the quality and long term effectiveness of the service users received.

The process of negotiating and agreeing performance measurement is often rushed. There are numerous examples of monitoring or contract officers working under pressure to bring in a performance measurement system to a tight timetable. They do not have the time available to think through what information is needed or useful. Some of the worst examples of measurement systems have been written by people who have little or no practical understanding of what it is they are trying to measure. They simply see it as a bureaucratic task. Such confusion can distort what the organisation does, create a confused picture or even lead to allegations that the organisation is "failing to perform".

Many managers also have experience of committing their agency to performance measures and indicators which they hope that they can meet as part of a making a "good impression" in a funding application or contract bid.

Good measurement needs careful thought and planning. It is useful to encourage people to decide what it is that they need to measure and how will they use the information.

CASE STUDY

PERFORMANCE INDICATORS: DIALS OR TIN OPENERS?

Neil Carter, writing in Policy and Politics in 1989 comments on a trend in central government to look for precise measures of performance when there are very few available. "It is helpful to think of performance indicators as being used either as dials or as tin openers. Implicit in the use of performance indicators as dials is the assumption that standards of performance are unambiguous, implicit in the use of performance indicators as tin openers is the assumption that performance is a contestable notion."

Thinking of indicators as dials assumes that the information is always clear and correct (like the temperature shown on a thermostat). However, there are few things that can always be measured with such accuracy. Thinking of performance indicators as tin openers recognises that most performance measurement systems of any value raise more questions than provide precise answers.

The design guide explained:

1 What is the service/project for?

Measures must be related to aims and objectives. What the service is for may seem obvious and need little discussion. However, people often have different ways of describing it which can sometimes lead to confusion and ambiguity. Frequently organisations drift into running lots of services and activities without properly agreeing aims and objectives.

It is useful at this stage to check tactfully that your view of what the service is for is the same as the bodies who fund or purchase the work. Often there is a clear agreement, but, considering the rate of internal change within most funding bodies it is possible that the officers responsible for monitoring your work only have a very vague understanding of the purpose of your organisation.

2 What values should influence it?

Values are the key principles and ways of working that are central to an organisation's existence. Possible values might include:

- Working with low income members of the community
- Equal opportunities in service delivery
- A commitment to client rights

Any measures used should be informed by the organisation's core values. It is important that performance indicators measure the things that an organisation regards as important and are distinctive about its style and method of working.

An adult education centre was required to produce performance indicators recording how many students were enrolled on its classes. The centre Director quickly realised that some courses such as French for holiday makers were very easy to fill whilst others required considerable hard work and effort. To recruit five people onto an adult literacy programme was a major achievement, but looked like a poor response on the monitoring returns. Discussions within the centre led to changes in the measures used. Rather than reporting on simple attendance the centre developed measures that reflected how much time it put into meeting value based priorities, eg. working with adults who had missed out on formal education.

3 What do we want to measure?

Informed by an understanding of the objectives and relevant values discussion can now focus on identifying possible measures. At this stage two points need to be considered:

- There is a practical limit on how much information can reasonably be collected without reducing the amount of time spent on the service itself. Focus on aiming for a limited number of key indicators that reflect what is really important rather than counting everything that can be counted.
- The process of monitoring may adversely affect the service itself. Callers to a confidential counselling help line might not appreciate having to answer lots of questions for the sake of the monitoring data or being contacted afterwards to discuss if use of the help line had led to a "positive outcome".

PERFORMANCE MEASUREMENT AS A DASHBOARD

Imagine trying to drive a car without the gauges on the dashboard. When you drive a car you need several indicators and measures to tell you at what speed that you are travelling at, the temperature of the engine, the amount of fuel remaining and warning lights to advise you of potential hazards. Too many gauges on the dashboard could confuse the driver and cause too many distractions from the task of driving the car.

One interesting approach to performance measurement is to use this metaphor to encourage people to think about what information they need to successfully manage and measure their work.

The staff team of a new neighbourhood safety project came up with the following dashboard for their project:

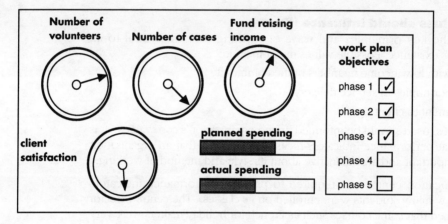

The process of trying to focus on a few core measures was an interesting one for the team. What really mattered? What results were important? What handful of measures were critical?

What would be on the dashboard for your organisation?

. . . .

. . . .

. . . .

. . . .

. . . .

. . . .

. . . .

. . . .

4 What are the possible measures and indicators?

After listing what is to be measured, the next stage is to decide upon the most appropriate and cost efficient method of collecting the required information, data and views.

The extra cost and time likely to be spent on collecting and compiling the information needs to be calculated. Is this a reasonable use of limited resources?

5 How will the information be used and interpreted?

How will you use the information? How will it feed into the management process? For example, monthly performance measures might tell you that the numbers attending the day centre are declining on Thursdays and Fridays. Who will be responsible for finding out what this means and acting on it before a trend becomes a problem?

How will your funders or purchasers use the information you give them? Do they review it in any organised way? Do they apply any objective judgment to it? A disability group was asked to compile statistics on how many people used its resource centre every day. The group was surprised to hear informally that the monitoring officer (who had little real knowledge of the group or its clients) regarded twenty users per day as being acceptable and that any fall below twenty was regarded as "poor performance". At no stage had this been discussed openly.

It is easy to interpret a simple piece of information in many different ways. Discussion should focus on what interpretation could be made of information and data collected under each indicator.

Most performance review systems do not have an explicit statement of what kind of interpretation will be placed on the collected information. It may be appropriate to agree to a regular review meeting to look at trends and patterns that emerge from indicators, discuss possible interpretations and identify future action.

PERFORMANCE INDICATORS - SOME "GOOD" EXAMPLES

There are numerous examples of performance indicators that have been thrown together in a hurry, that only count the things that are easy to count and ignore the things that are important. The indicators listed below are possible "positive" ones which could meet meet an organisation's specific objectives and values.

1. Staff Training and Development

A simple indicator showing the average number of training days attended by an agency's staff. A second indicator could record the total amount spent on staff development as a percentage of the total salary budget.

These indicators could be used as a measure of good management practice and also of a commitment to maintain high professional standards.

2. Consultation with users

An indicator that records the total number of staff hours or days spent on consulting with users, non-users and past-users on the quality of services and in the planning of future services.

3. Independent "audit" of cases

A review of randomly selected closed cases by an outside expert to evaluate the accuracy of casework and to discuss with the caseworker and also the client the effectiveness of the approach taken.

4. An indicator of "unmet" need

Compiling a list of occasions when an agency has had to turn people away, either because the service has reached a capacity level or because the needs expressed could not be met by the agency's current services.

5. A report on specific measures taken to improve services in line with agreed policies

A report on work undertaken to improve the agency services in line with policy directions. For example, an agency could report on the following:

Policy Objective	Action taken
To improve access for people with disabilities	During this quarter we have: • Met with the council's disability adviser to review access. • Established the cost of an appropriate wheelchair lift. • Met with local disabled groups to discuss access needs.
To work in a way that reflects	• We have reviewed all purchasing policies.
Good environmental practice	• We have arranged for a heating audit to be carried out.

6. Innovative or developmental projects

An agency that is committed to finding new solutions to problems could record, as an indicator, what new projects or activities it is involved in as a measure of its innovative work and developmental role.

A CHECKLIST FOR USING PERFORMANCE MEASURES

Related to a specific function or activity

It makes sense that measures and indicators directly relate to the way in which the organisation is structured. Measures and indicators should not cut across staff teams or budget heads. It should be clear which part of the organisation or which individual is responsible for managing the activity that the performance indicator reports on. Measures could be linked to:

Organisational structures and functions.
Measures could be based on the work structures of teams and units so that each team would have ownership of the specific measures.

Specific plans.
Several organisations design measures and indicators that relate to goals and targets set out in business plans or work plans. This can give some meaning to such plans. It is useful way of making sure that the plan once agreed is not forgotten.

Contract or funding obligations.
Linking measures to the requirements of service agreements or contracts is an effective way of strengthening the contract management process. It will provide useful early warning systems to alert both the provider and purchaser to any problem areas.

The following ten points are a useful checklist when agreeing and reviewing measures.

Are the Measures:

☐ Related to a specific function or activity?

☐ Agreed in advance?

☐ Capable of being managed or improved?

☐ Easy to collect?

☐ Measurable?

☐ Easy to understand?

☐ Reflecting an even and total picture?

☐ Linked into planning?

☐ Related to values and objectives

☐ Cost effective?

Capable of control or of being improved

There is no point in being measured against something which the organisation is not actually responsible for or is not capable of improving or managing better.

A voluntary group working with young homeless people is not responsible for the numbers of homeless young people in its area (in fact their work might well establish that there are more young homeless people than previously estimated).

Using the numbers of young homeless people in a town as an indicator of performance (as opposed to an indicator of need) is pointless and unfair.

Changes in the social security system might mean that a welfare rights worker has less opportunity to win a direct increase in a person's benefit, however hard she works. So using "successful outcomes" (i.e. winning a case) as an indicator might well provide interesting information, but, not necessarily on the performance of a welfare rights service.

It is worthwhile to ask "can we actually improve in any way the performance that is being monitored or is it entirely dependent on external circumstances beyond our influence?".

Measurable

Performance reviews can only focus on things that are measurable in either quantity or quality terms. Are there aspects of the service which are important but, are particularly difficult to measure? Or where the costs or time involved in collecting data would be too much? Could the process of collecting information be objected to or cause suspicion amongst clients or users?

Reflects an even and total picture

Some parts of an organisation are easier to measure than other parts. There is a danger of only focussing on the tangible (...how many people and at what cost?) aspects of the organisation and ignoring things that are intangible. Often intangible things are about the way an organisation works - does it consult its clients, does it give choices?

The range of measures and indicators agreed should reflect the full scope, depth and purpose of the organisation.

Related to values and objectives

Do the performance indicators measure what the organisation (and hopefully its funders) regards as important about what it does and how it does it?

Agreed in advance

Performance measures should not be imposed retrospectively (eg. a funding body suddenly asking for figures for a previous year). It is only fair to agree performance measures at the start of a project or funding agreement. This allows the organisation to design and implement systems to collect information and by monitoring performance throughout the period it will be able to intervene to improve performance. Measurement needs to be central feature of contract and funding negotiation.

Easy to collect

There is much more likelihood of a performance measurement system being effective and accurate if the recording system is easy to use. Whenever possible any recording system should be integrated into current procedures such as booking systems, casework record systems or diaries rather than staff having to fill in separate monitoring systems.

Easy to understand

The information collected together should be in an easy to read and simple format. There is a tendency with some funding bodies to restrict information to a few core statistics to make analysis and compilation easy.

Any statistical information should be collected in such a way that, if it is necessary, it can be accompanied by some commentary which describes any significant factors (eg. "...February figures are lower than usual because the building was closed for redecoration work for three days").

Linked into planning

There should be a link between collecting information about performance and making decisions about an organisation's short and long term future. Trends and data gleaned from the performance measurement system should be used to inform decisions about budgets and future plans (for example if a group is unable to meet its performance standard that the office is always open from 10.00 to 16.00 it would need to consider how it organises staff cover).

Cost effective

How much will it cost to record and collect the information? How much staff time will it take up? Is the value that will be gained from collecting information about performance worth the cost and time involved in collecting it? One useful measure is how much time is spent collecting, collating and producing performance measurement information.

PERFORMANCE MEASUREMENT AS A RULER

A ruler in a classroom can have several uses. It can be used to measure items and develop learning about size. But children can also use it to inflict pain on each other by using it as a weapon.

Performance measurement systems often have this dual use. They can be used to provide valuable information that makes us think, question and understand what we do in a positive way. Or alternatively, they can be used as a threat or means to gather evidence to punish people or organisations. Inappropriate performance measurement leads to people playing the system - doing only what is necessary to achieve a good score on the indicator to avoid negative sanctions.

If they are to be used to create learning and development then there needs to be a positive commitment by all parties to openness, sensible interpretation and communication between parties.

TYPES OF MEASURES AND INDICATORS

Unit Cost

Cost of Service.
Number of times used.

If a home visiting service cost
£6,000 each month and in a
particular month carried out 120
visits the unit cost would be £50.
Unit costs only make sense if
every unit is likely to be relatively similar.
If one home visit takes 10 minutes and another takes
3 hours, then the figure of £50 becomes a fairly
meaningless average.

Cost of overheads

Amount of money spent
on running costs and
administration as opposed
to direct service costs.

Assumes that the agency's
financial procedures are able to
report this information in an
accurate and true manner. Can
lead to "creative accounting" whereby
costs are hidden to achieve the desired result.

Occupancy

Optimum Use.
Actual use.

If an arts centre had workshop
space for three sessions per day its
optimum use level would be sixty
sessions in a four week period.
If, in one period, it was used for
fifty sessions then its occupancy
rate would be 83%. Optimum use rates
work best in situations where a service
has a fixed capacity point such as the
number of beds in a hostel.

NOTES

....
....
....
....
....

TYPES OF MEASURES AND INDICATORS

Take up rate

Number of
clients, enquiries
or users

The number of service users are,
recorded and often put into categories by
client profile (age, sex etc.), type of
issue or time taken to deal with.
This can provide useful information about
trends in service use provided interpretation
is fair. This indicator only records how busy
the service is rather than how effective it is.

Performance against agreed standard

Number of times
that a service has
met or failed to
meet an agreed
minimum level

This measure is often used in a quality
assurance framework. An
agreed "benchmark" is set, eg.
"all initial referrals will be
dealt with in four days". Performance
against the standard is then recorded.
This can be used as a negative indicator
to identify when a service is not
working to the agreed standard.

Performance against an agreed plan

Reporting on the
completion of agreed
objectives and
tasks

A plan of work is agreed
with written objectives and
time scales. This can be useful
in activities of a developmental
nature eg. community work. One
possible way to avoid the plan becoming
too rigid is to build in flexibility
by only planning for say 70% of available time.

NOTES

....
....
....
....
....
....

TYPES OF MEASURES AND INDICATORS

User feedback

Collation of user
opinions, reactions
and surveys

The organised collection of the views and
reactions of users. Thought needs to be
given as to who should collect the information
and also to collecting the views of ex-users.

Communications audit

A survey of an
organisation's
users to measure their
knowledge of its
services and activities.

A review of how effectively
the organisation informs
users about it's work: Simple
direct questions eg. "Is there
a complaints procedure?"

User panels

Establishing small
groups of users, and
clients to comment on
services.

A more open evaluation technique.
Panels act as a point of reference for
reviewing the service.In market research
these groups are known as focus groups and are
usually led by external consultants.

Case audits

Internal and external
analysis and reviews of a
limited number of cases
to ensure that they have been
managed in line with agreed practice.

Audits need to have a clear
standards of what is good
practice. Cases could be
audited by managers, other staff
or independent experts.

NOTES

....
....
....
....
....
....
....

TYPES OF MEASURES AND INDICATORS

Follow up reviews

A random sample of past users and clients are contacted to comment on their experience of the service.

Some agencies have developed techniques for keeping in touch with past users and tracking their experience.

Matching expectations with actual experience

The organised recording of users initial hopes expectations about a service contrasted against their experience of using it.

Some training agencies ask trainees to record what they hope to learn from a course. These statements are stored away until end of the course. They are then asked to indicate if their original expectations have been met.

Policy Indicators

A positive report on what actions and resource allocations have been given to advancing specific policy commitments in the past six months?

One agency reports on how much time and money it had spent on responding to a policy. For example, what did it do to implement its anti-racist policy?

NOTES

....
....
....
....
....
....
....

TYPES OF MEASURES AND INDICATORS

Complaint Analysis
Complaints made are analysed
and grouped by issue and location.

This can provide useful information.
There is an argument that suggests that
the management of complaints can be
regarded as a positive indicator of good
management practice. It is possible that
agencies do not get complaints because
the systems and staff discourage complaints
and that users do not bother to complain.
They have no confidence in the ability of
the organisation to respond properly.

Referral Indicators
A report on how users
first made contact with the service.

An indicator of how users found
out about a service by referral routes.

No service given
A report on the occasions
when the agency has had
to turn potential users away.

Recording demands for a service
which were not met. Often this
information is not collected.

Lost opportunities
A review of initiatives that
were not followed up due to
lack of resources. "...No available
staff time prevented us from....".

Often new possibilities are ignored
or forgotten about. This can provide
useful information for future planning.

NOTES

....
....
....
....
....
....
....

A ONE PAGE MONITORING FORM

A version of this form was used by a community health project to report on its performance on a quarterly basis.

Summary of key objectives for this quarter

- To continue to run the training programme, resource centre and information services to agreed targets.
- To develop self help groups to be established in the key priority areas.
- To develop new initiatives project with young people.
- To investigate the feasibility of a health shop on the estate.

Summary of activity output measures

- 87 people attended six two day HIV courses.
- 47 people attended three one day courses (two courses cancelled).
- 117 people have used the resource centre. 176 brief information calls.
- 2000 copies of new alcohol awareness pack distributed.
- Three Health mailings sent to 260 organisations/contacts.
- Speakers provided at 17` classes, courses and local groups.
- Five self help support groups in session (total participants 40).
- The working group on health shop met three times and produced first report.

Reaction and feedback

- Course evaluation : 73% of participants rated good to excellent.
- Three month course follow up evaluation being carried out.
- 56 requests for information from health mailing.

Significant Trends

- Estimate that at least 75% of our users are women.
- Noticeable increase in enquiries about access to counselling services.

Outcome/results identified in this period

- Three of the support groups are now capable of meeting with little direct support from the project.
- Follow up groups from two training courses have met - a summary of action carried by participants has been prepared.
- General Practitioners advisory group has commented that many of their patients who have used the project have a greater understanding of health issues.
- Health Purchaser has given initial support to our feasibility study on work with carers - full proposal to next meeting.
- Inter agency partnership group on drugs now permanently established independent of us.

Notes

Long term sickness of project worker has meant no progress on new initiatives project with young people
The project has spent five working days on convening users consultation groups - work not in service agreement or work plan - but requested as an urgent priority by the heath authority.

MEASURING AT DIFFERENT LEVELS

One structure for designing measures is to divide an activity into four areas and devise a limited number of indicators and measures for each area.

Take the example of a campaign to recruit volunteers to work in local community projects. Its overall objective is to "recruit and select forty suitable people to become local volunteers". This objective was to be met through a week long public exhibition leading on to follow up interviews, training and placement.

Activity/output measures	The exhibition was open for 64 hours. It cost £345. It was attended by 412 people.
Reaction measures	186 of those that attended filled in an evaluation form of which 76% were satisfied or impressed by the exhibition.
Impact measures	78 people expressed an interest in becoming a volunteer. 57 people attended a follow up interview of which 49 people were progressed on to the volunteer training programme.
Outcome measures	36 people took part in a three day volunteer training programme. Three months later 32 people have been placed as volunteers in community projects giving an average input of seven hours per week.

The following five points are useful in using this structure for designing measures:

- As you work through from outputs to outcome the process of measurement becomes looser. It is usually possible to have tight indicators to record the volume of what is going on. People's immediate reaction to it also can be recorded through complaints and feedback measures although this often needs careful management and interpretation. Impact and outcome measures often need follow thorough measurement, are often more judgmental and need intelligent interpretation.

- The impact measure is a measure of what happens directly as a consequence of the activity. This could include what the user or client did, what action they took or what response they made.

- In any information gathering system there is a danger of over measurement. In this example it would be possible to identity many other possible measures - how long did the average visitor spend at the exhibition? what was the gender, age or race profile of the visitors? what did people think of the training, why did some people not progress on? and how do the managers of the community projects evaluate the placed volunteers? are all other questions that could usefully be asked. The key issue in designing measures is to make sure that there are a limited number of measures focused on the important aspects of the operation that effectively tell you what is happening and are the objectives being achieved. Over measurement is costly and shifts resources from doing the work to measuring it. Effective measurement needs discipline and clarity of focus.

- A useful way of using this structure is to start by recording the objectives and listing the outcomes that you are interested in. The process of writing down the objectives and outcomes first, sometimes shows up fuzzy or vague thinking about why you are doing something and what you want to achieve. Once they are clear you can then design indicators and measures to pick up the actions and steps that you believe are important in achieving the outcome. Starting with the output can lead to narrow thinking and a limited focus on volume and activity. This narrow thinking can lead to a measurement system that is production rather than result orientated and obscures outcomes by regarding them as secondary or incidental.

- Outcomes do take time to develop. This does mean that the measurement system does need to take a longer term view. How long will depend on each particular instance. For example it might be interesting in this case to find out how many of the volunteers are still working, say, six months after the training, but it is questionable if the exhibition and placement activity would have much, if any, effect on whether volunteers stayed beyond this time.

A QUESTION OF INTERPRETATION

Two information offices provide a similar service and with the same levels of staffing, opening times and community profile. A performance measurement system was developed using two indicators:

How many people used the centre in a month.

The average length of each interview.

The figures reveal that Centre A had 75 clients calling in for initial interviews and that the average interview lasted 10 minutes while staff at Centre B saw 38 clients and the average interview lasted 30 minutes.

The following, very different interpretations could be placed on this information.

- "Centre A is obviously busier as it sees more people."

- "Centre A is better than Centre B as it can deal with more people in an efficient (i.e. quick) way."

- "Centre B is probably disorganised as it takes on average 20 minutes longer to provide the same information as centre A."

- "Centre B gives callers more time. People probably get a much more personalised and responsive service than at centre A."

- "I suspect that many of Centre A's callers are repeat visits i.e. the same people coming back again. If more time was spent with them initially, as probably happens at Centre B, it would be more efficient in the longer term."

- "On average Centre A staff conducted 12.5 hours of initial interviews. Centre B staff conducted 19 hours of interviews. That means that Centre B staff work harder and are busier."

This example shows just how easy it is to draw from a relatively simple piece of information very different and, in fact, contradictory conclusions. The collection of average times tell little, if anything about the quality of the interview and the long term effectiveness of it.

In looking at any set of information our interpretation of it is usually based upon sets of assumptions and personal beliefs about what we think is the right way to do something.

Clearly it is important to clarify how managers, funders and staff will interpret whatever information a performance indicator produces. What assumptions will they be making in "judging" the information?

CHAPTER 3

Value For Money-Making Comparisons

As money continues to get tighter, all public funded agencies are under pressure to show that their activities provide "value for money". Value for money or "VFM" started life in accountancy and moved into the turbulent world of funders, policy makers and service providers.

A Chartered Institute of Public Finance and Accountancy publication on Value For Money sums up the confusion and misuse of the term "value for money".

* *"Few slogans can have been so widely adopted and yet be so misunderstood as "value for money". It has been variously used as a political rallying call; as a euphemism for expenditure reductions; and to imply quality and cheapness in goods as diverse as motor cars and washing up liquids.*

It was coined from within the public sector finance discipline to give expression to a prime economic goal of most public service organisations."

With central government's commitment to making comparisons between service providers through league tables and Citizen Charters it is clear that proving "value for money", with all of its limitations, will remain a constant feature of the relationship between public and voluntary bodies.

* with permission Chartered Institute of Public Finance and Accountancy

WHAT VFM MEANS

Most definitions of value for money focus on three "E"s:

Economy

- How does the cost of the service compare to the costs of similar services?
- Are monies and resources allocated and used on a sensible economic basis?
- Are wage levels, rent levels, purchasing policies and on costs managed in a sound and thrifty way?

Efficiency

- Is the service well managed?
- Does it use resources in an prudent way?
- Does the service operate in a way that achieves the maximum output?
- Could more be achieved if it were better organised?

Effectiveness

- Does the activity work short term - medium term and longer term?
- Did it achieve its intended objectives?
- Are the short and long term benefits that the service delivers worth the investment?
- The features of value for money can easily be applied to the inputs, outputs and outcomes model described in chapter two.

CASE STUDY

EFFICIENT OR EFFECTIVE?

In February 1995 the Audit Commission published a study, "In the line of fire" which looked at value for money in the fire service. It drew attention to what it described as a "perverse incentive" in the national funding formula for fire brigades.

The Standing Spending Assessments which determine the amount each fire authority receives from central government is based on the number of fires and false alarm calls a fire brigade responds to. The purpose of the funding is to reduce harm caused by fire to people and property. The formula works in such a way that for every fire a fire brigade prevents through effective fire prevention work it loses money through the assessment. It penalises local brigades that have run successful and cost effective prevention work.

INPUTS, OUTPUTS, OUTCOMES
AND VALUE FOR MONEY

Is it economic?

Does the amount of resource allocated make good economic sense?
How does the cost of the activity compare?

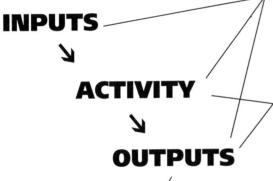

INPUTS

ACTIVITY

Is it efficient?

Is it efficient? Given the level of input provided is the output sufficient? If the activity was better organised could more outputs be delivered for the same (or less) input?

OUTPUTS

OUTCOMES

Is it effective?

Does it work?
Did it meet the original objectives?
Are the outcomes worth the input?

HOW IT WORKS IN PRACTICE

Is it economic?

Commentators have observed that most value for money studies rarely get beyond the first question - is the service funded on an economic basis? Even that issue can degenerate into simply finding ways of making short term reductions in expenditure that can have a long term cost.

Many organisations have either consistently under estimated the costs of their activities or because of lack of funds failed to properly invest and have ran services at very low cost. Employing a staff member to do a job and not giving them the resources to do it is not a sensible way to manage. Doing things "on the cheap" does not necessarily mean doing them on a sensible economic basis.

Is it efficient?

Just because a service is ran in an efficient way it does not mean it is effective in delivering the "right services to the right people".

The link between efficiency and effectiveness is an interesting one. Management writers such as Peter Drucker, have stressed that unless an organisation thinks strategically about its purpose it can very easily do entirely the wrong thing in a very efficient manner.

Is it effective?

Economy and efficiency can usually be measured in the short term (eg. within a financial year). The effectiveness of a service, particularly a one involved in providing some element of social care or community development might not become apparent for a number of years.

Preventative work often has a considerable initial cost, however, it can only be evaluated if the long term cost of not doing it is estimated.

A further complication is that there is not always a direct line between outputs and outcomes. An organisation might produce high quality services which are used in an entirely different way by a local community. They place a value on that service, but it is different from the one originally intended.

If a service is effective (i.e. it is of a consistent quality that meets people's needs) then it can be assumed that it will possibly attract new users or that existing users will keep using it and that their expectations of it will rise. Being effective can mean that a service is used more and therefore costs (either on a unit or an overall basis) are likely to rise and thus the "economic" element could change.

If a community centre is well managed and is responding to local needs in a popular and effective way its resources will come under greater strain. At the very least, it will need more cleaning, maintaining, administration and management. Its equipment will be used more often and will probably need servicing and repairing more often than a quieter centre.

Making judgments

Value for money studies are used to provide information for making judgments. A value can only be established if it is possible to find some benchmarks or alternatives to make relevant comparisons. The issue of comparisons is fraught with difficulties. All figures need to be read in some sort of context. The government's decision to publish lists of school examination results was roundly criticised for lacking any context in local situations.

Making comparisons or league tables is a difficult and sometimes controversial exercise. No two service providers are ever identical either in terms of their available resources, organisation and objectives or in the external environment in which they operate. History, user profiles, local socio-economic factors are all variables which make finding a comparison difficult.

Three types of comparisons that can be made usually include:
* Comparing current performance to past performance
  Are more outputs delivered this year compared to last year?
  Has performance improved or declined?

* Comparing the costs to a similar provider
  Do similar organisations manage to provide the same services at
  less cost? If the service was contracted out or provided by someone else
  would it provide better value for money?

* Comparing it to a different type of intervention
  Could the same value be achieved by providing a different (and possibly
  cheaper) service? If a a youth project switched from centre based work to
  outreach work would it be more economic, efficient and effective?

Perhaps a more relevant comparison is the cost of providing the service and not providing it, comparing the short term savings of not doing it as opposed to potential medium and longer term costs.

The following issues are useful in considering the relevance and application of a value for money exercise:

* Can a relevant comparison be made?
* Do all the organisations which we are being compared to collect figures in the same way?
* Do we work with the same users and aim for the same outcome?
* Do we have some mechanism process for identifying longer term outcomes?

ADDED VALUE

A spin off term from value for money is the concept of added value or "additionality" as it is occasionally called. Added value is what your organisation adds to the inputs it receives.

Examples of added value include:

People's time
An obvious example of added value in the voluntary sector is the use of volunteers to provide extra services that complement and extend the requirements of the contract. One charity received a contract of £150000 to work with families in crisis. As well as the paid staff team a group of volunteers were on hand to assist and compliment the staff team. Picking an equivalent hourly rate and multiplying it by the average number of volunteer hours donated in the week led to a claim that the charity added £11000 of value to the contract.

The same argument could be made for the contribution that management committees make.

Special insight or skill
One arts agency suggested that its track record of creative and innovative ideas and dynamic ways of working added value to the input. Assembling an equivalent organisation from scratch would be very costly.

Efficient management
Well managed organisations with low costs and good resources add value. A project housed in an organisation with other similar projects could lead to effective sharing of resources and possibly good co-operation and liaison which could lead to added value.

Special knowledge or contacts
Having local knowledge, local credibility and contacts is often taken for granted, but could be argued that they represent an important asset base in an organisation. Such knowledge and insight could not be established overnight and would require considerable investment.

Leverage to other funds
An increasingly common approach to added value is to suggest that the investment of one fund will secure other funds. A charitable trust fund could be persuaded to donate funds to a project to develop and complement the work paid for by a local authority contract. This represents "added value" to the local authority's expenditure.

Added value is not a water tight objective concept. In practice, it is an advocate's tool that can be used to make an argument to advance a particular case.

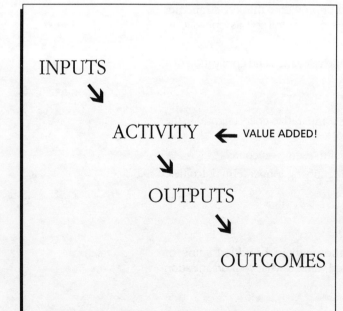

A PRACTICAL EXAMPLE OF ADDED VALUE

The East Side Centre ran an alternative to custody project working with up to twenty young people. It cost £80,000 per year to fund the scheme.

Asked to prove that it provided "value for money", it considered the following.

Who could it compare itself against?

How do we judge our work?

The centre was unable to identify an exact comparison. Every other centre or project it compared itself to varied in some significant way (size, type of work, client group, geography etc.). However, it was able to make the following points about the economic and efficient aspects of VFM:

- Its staff costs accounted for 65% of its operating costs. Salary grade levels were the same as those in similar statutory functions.

- The centre spent very little on management and administrative functions. Its "on costs" or overheads figures worked out to be about 19%. In other similar projects run by national agencies or statutory bodies the figure would be more like 30%.

- The centre argued that it "added value" to the income it received from its service agreement. The centre used volunteers to work alongside paid workers. It calculated that the equivalent replacement cost of voluntary effort was at least £10,000 per year. So, in effect, it added £10,000 worth of value to the £80,000 it received from its service agreement.

The centre tried to gather evidence of the short and long term effectiveness of its work. It made the following points:

- Providing an average of twelve places a week for forty eight weeks at a total cost of £80,000 gave it a unit cost of £139 per young person per week.

- For this figure to have any meaning it had to be put into some sort of context. The centre suggested that for many of the young people with whom it worked the alternative to the centre's programme would be a period of custody. Consulting government figures it found that the average unit cost of a place in a young offenders institution worked out at £450 per week.

- However, these figures showed little about the actual effectiveness of its work. Agreeing what was an effective outcome was not straight forward. One possible success outcome it identified was that a young person would not re-offend within a twelve month period.

- The only available figures that the centre had were patchy, but, they did show that young people who had attended had a 10% higher success rate than equivalent figures for a custodial sentence.

- The centre was able to use these figures to argue that the centre did provide value for money, that it added value to the inputs it received and had a higher rate of success than more expensive alternatives.

CHAPTER 4

Defining Quality

In the 1990s one of the biggest management and organisational focuses has been around quality. A whole quality movement has grown up. Most major companies and organisations have launched quality management and improvement programmes, committed themselves to listening to their customers and have worked to win external quality awards.

In the public sector, central government departments and agencies have adopted charters setting out standards. Local councils and health authorities have developed several initiatives. Major "cultural" change projects have been mounted, quality assurance units set up, public consultation increased and a much greater emphasis placed on responding to newly named "customers". Several national and local voluntary agencies are also committing themselves to quality initiatives or being required by funders or purchasers to do so.

Making sense of the quality movement is not easy. Management bookshelves are stacked with different approaches, definitions and heavily marketed perfect solutions.

It is possible to identify three different strands in the quality movement:

Quality Control
Quality control is not new. Most manufacturing and service enterprises have developed audits and inspections to check that what has been produced or delivered conforms to specification. Quality control is reactive as it checks on things after they have been done.

Quality Assurance
The emphasis of quality assurance is to identify and build on good practice and then set out minimum standards that users should always be able to expect. The assumption behind quality assurance is that if we can ensure that the key activities and processes always operate to a clear standard then the organisation should always produce a consistent level of quality. The quality award, BS5750 (or IS EN BS 9000 as it is properly called) is one approach to quality assurance.

Total Quality Management

Total Quality Management (TQM) has its roots in manufacturing industries in Japan and North America. It is a collection of management systems, working practices (such as teamwork) and processes that aims to focus an organisation on continually improving and building strong co-operative relationships. This ensures that everyone involved in the system is committed to meeting and exceeding customer needs and expectations. To be successful requires considerable internal change in how the organisation works.

There are a lot of instances of these initiatives being launched with great fanfare and promise only to fade away or be sidelined as the organisation moves on to something else. Often quality programmes are criticised for being driven from the top by senior managers. They are also criticised for generating inflexible rules and systems that frustrate people who are simply trying to do a job.

However, quality initiatives have the potential to clarify what is quality, create open and lively dialogue with their users, build on good practice and focus attention on the lasting quality of the work rather than the quantity of it.

Experience of developing quality programmes in several agencies suggests two issues that seem central to whether any quality programme succeeds or fails:

A clear definition of what quality is

Pinpointing the features and ingredients that define quality in a specific service or activity is often hard work. It is easy to write quality standards for what you are currently doing without ever checking to see if they are what people want, need and think are important. Most organisations have very few techniques for finding out what the individuals who could use, currently use or have used their services actually want or think about it.

A management style able to see it through

How a quality initiative is launched, the processes involved in it and the degree of participation involved do seem to to have a critical impact on its success. Managers need to be able to manage and initiate a project that will require extra work, create a feeling of ownership throughout and be able to manage the organisational changes involved in it.

A GUIDE TO QUALITY SPEAK

Total Quality Management

A management process that focuses on identifying how all aspects of a process (suppliers, managers, front line staff and support staff) directly contribute to the quality of a product or service. It stresses the importance of team work, systems, communication and continual improvement to ensure that quality standards are always met.

Quality Assurance

Quality Assurance is a term increasingly being used in the field of social and health care. Essentially it involves designing and planning services to ensure that they are able to perform in such a way that guarantees that the service will always meet the agreed standard. Systems and indicators need to be developed to ensure that the service consistently operates to its agreed standards. Quality Assurance should be a "pro-active" management process.

Quality Control

Quality Control is a process which is directed at checking and inspecting a process after it has been completed and ensuring that it is acceptable. It is more of a "reactive" or "fire fighting" process than quality assurance.

The Cost of Quality

The direct and indirect cost of making mistakes and having to correct work later.

BS5750, EN 29000 and IS9000

Externally accredited certification which shows that an organisation has in place systems and processes to measure and ensure a quality product or service. BS5750 is the UK standard, EN 29000 the European one and IS9000 the international one. All follow the same pattern and format.

Statistical Process Control

A preventative method to ensure that at each step of a process staff check their own work against agreed standards to ensure that it conforms to standard. Statistical Process Control should give staff the "feedback" on what is happening so that they can take action if things start to fall below standard.

Quality Circles

A management and communication strategy, originally developed in Japanese industry, whereby, groups of workers meet on a regular basis to identify ways in which services can be improved.

360 DEGREE EVALUATION

A resource centre decided to develop quality standards for its work. It decided to list the people with whom it had a relationship. This is sometimes called a 'stakeholders analysis'. It soon became apparent that it had many different kinds of relationships, all with different expectations.

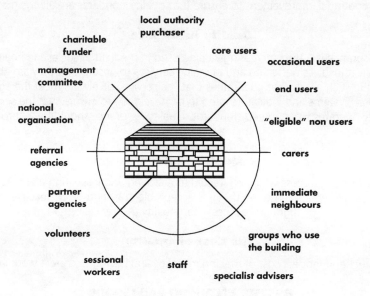

It identified five different kinds of relationships all of which would need some input into the quality programme.

Primary users – people whom the organisation was set up to help and support. This group would have significant say in the quality process.

Secondary users – other people who also benefit from the organisation, but do not use it for its 'core business'.

Internal relationships – staff, management committee and volunteers who will have expectations of each other.

Client relationships – funders, purchasers and referrals who may a financial relationship with the organisation.

External relationships – people such as neighbours who do not have a direct relationship to the centre but are affected by it.

PRIVATE VERSUS PUBLIC QUALITY

In many discussions with individuals in the public and voluntary sector the comparisons to successful high street retailers is often made. Their much vaunted success at creating top quality services is proclaimed as an example. But is it such a useful example? From a quality point of view, here's a quick comparison between the fast food restaurant and a local community centre:

Fast food restaurant	**Local community centre**
Tight specification and control of the whole business process Everyone involved - suppliers, staff and customers stand to benefit.	Success depends on lots of the inputs of and cooperation of lots of different people some of who are not financially connected.
Few variables - very limited menu	Lots of different formal and informal activities taking place throughout the week.
All customers know what to expect and what they want from the centre. There will probably be limited interaction with customers - sale takes less than a minute.	People want very different things. What an OAP wants different from a teenager. "Customers" can be users, volunteers, carers for other users and involved in managing the centre.
Only in one business.	In lots of businesses - advice, youth work, social care, etc. community action, recreation
Has clear financial measures - return on investment, sales targets and profit/loss.	Not in it to make a profit.

DEFINING QUALITY

A first glance at the material and literature concerning quality could suggest that it is a very mechanical and even bureaucratic process. Formal quality standards, an emphasis on documentation and procedures could lead to the conclusion that quality is all about systems and not much about people's expectations, needs and wants.

All too often, managers operating at great distance have drawn up standards and procedures which simply reinforce current practice or are designed for what they think are the quality elements of an activity. There has been no consultation, dialogue or discussion to find out what is important to the people the activity is supposed to be designed for. Examples of this are particularly common in the public sector. In their book, Managing Public Services, Common, Flynn and Mellon describe the experience of a Department of Social Security office which went to great lengths to ensure that all callers were seen within two minutes. After a time they realised that being seen within two minutes was not a critical factor for many of their "customers". A survey showed that factors such as the privacy of the interview were regarded as being much more important than the speed at which they were seen. Investing in time and effort in meeting and sustaining a level of "quality" that is not relevant or important is wasteful, frustrating and often generates cynicism from staff and users.

Before rushing into any quality programme careful and often long term work needs to be invested to establish what the people for whom the service or activity is designed think is important about what it docs and how it docs it. Three questions need focusing on:

- **Who is it for?**

- **What is their view of the current service?**

- **What does quality mean to them?**

These questions can provoke considerable debate.

Several organisations have had to distinguish between different kinds of users. Some have a primary relationship to the organisation whilst others have a secondary one. For example, a family centre had to decide which of their potential users it should listen to most. Was it the children who they worked with or their families and carers who were often involved, was it the teachers and social workers who referred cases or was it the local authority who purchased the service? There may well be some considerable difference between what different parties see as "quality". Their investment in it and expectations of quality may need careful discussion and negotiation.

Some of the hype about quality implies that the organisation needs to be entirely driven by users; almost as if "a quality service is one which does whatever a user wants". In most cases this is an entirely unrealistic expectation. The need to plan services, the diversity of user needs, legal, professional and contractual obligations often means that in reality such commitments are merely rhetorical slogans. A more practical view is that the organisation needs to be clear about what its goals are and what business it is in and then develop a relationship to the people who use it that is responsive, informed and continually listens to and learns from them.

The process of finding out what users think is "quality" is usually a demanding one. It requires considerable effort and ability to find ways of getting feedback, opinions and views. Most organisational systems for finding out users' views are fairly rudimentary and accidental. There is often a lack of skills in carrying out research, evaluation and in listening to people.

In several organisations management and staff attitudes need tackling. In some the view that "we know best" dominates - an over confident belief in professional judgment and training. In others there is a kind of organisational arrogance. One manager confessed to "not bothering with consumer research any more as their criticisms of what we do are always the same every year". Often the organisation is so confident that it is doing the "right thing" it adopts a tunnel vision. One section manager in the headquarters of a national charity commented how it was "surprising how many people kept phoning up for the wrong things".

A key learning point is that the end objective is not about finding out what the "user view is". There are sometimes as many different views about what is important as there are users. An effective quality process needs to be informed by a continual dialogue and discussion with users, past users, people who refer work, carers and other interested parties. Either through agreeing a consensus or by resolving conflicts it then needs to arrive at a view of what are the main features and factors that make up quality for each particular service or activity.

Defining quality needs to be more than doing a survey or only using one technique. One housing association commissioned researchers to carry out an extensive survey of tenant views. A lengthy survey was designed, piloted and carried out. Ten months later the findings were presented to staff meetings and management committees. Despite the cost and work involved in producing it, the report failed to provide any useful information. What conclusions could be drawn from the statement that 69% of respondents rated the maintenance system highly when the system had been reorganised just after the survey and that at least 20% of the respondents had either been rehoused or had moved in the past year. What criteria were they using to judge it? Did a majority view in favour discount the opinions and experience of the 21% who did not see it positively?

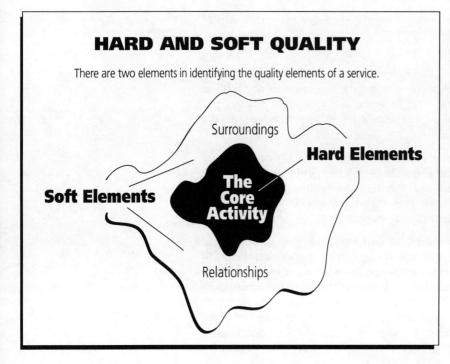

HARD AND SOFT QUALITY

There are two elements in identifying the quality elements of a service.

Surroundings

Hard Elements

Soft Elements

The Core Activity

Relationships

HARD AND SOFT QUALITY

One idea is to think of a service as having two elements, both of which are of value and are important in determining quality. Getting both issues in balance is important.

The hard elements relate to the core activity. This is the obvious service or product that the user expects and receives.

Quality factors for the hard elements include:
• Did it meet original expectations?

• Did it work?

• Was it worth the cost and time involved?

• Was it accurate?

• Was it competently delivered?

• Does it conform to the original specification?

The soft elements might be harder to identify and specify. They include the atmosphere, relationship and way in which the core activity is delivered. Sometimes these factors are called the "feel good factor".

Quality factors for the soft elements include:
• How was I made to feel?

• Was I involved, informed and consulted?

• Was it personal to me?

• Did I like how I was treated?

Several private companies have found that how customers are treated is as of equal importance (if not greater) in their memory than the product itself. One computer company found that the intangible factors (such as relationship between the sales rep and the customer) and factors such as the "user friendliness" of the machine were critical.

Sometimes the softer elements are worked on to the exclusion of the core activity. One local authority manager commented "We went overboard about packaging the service - one stop shops, training front line staff in customer care and a new logo - all good ideas on their own. The problem is that the core service is badly designed, badly managed and badly delivered. All of these new initiatives have merely provided a temporary camouflage".

The following seven points are based on the positive experience of several agencies in defining quality:

1 The more techniques that can be used the better

There are a range of techniques possible - group discussions, focus groups, consultation meetings, complaints analysis, interviews, follow up contacts and feedback sessions are just some examples. It is sensible not to treat any one technique as being entirely objective or scientific.

One agency found that they obtained a very different picture when a feedback form was handed to the user by someone the user did not know or have a lot of contact with rather than by the person who provided the service to them. Users were reluctant to give negative feedback to someone with whom they had a relationship and on whom they were dependent.

The more techniques that are used the more likely it is that you will be able to pick out themes and interpret findings in a useful way.

2 Welcome diversity

The objective is not to establish what all users think all of the time. The director of a housing association commented that "Six years ago we decided to create a space for tenants on our committees. Most of the time the places were empty, but when a tenant did come it used to scare me that the rest of the committee assumed that whenever they spoke they somehow represented the views of all of our tenants. The tenant was supposed to represent the views of 200 people aged from 20 to 80 scattered over a 45 mile radius. It was impossible. Now we use lots of different channels, but most especially all staff are encouraged to listen and feed things back. Often we get a mixture of views. It is our job to pick out themes and plan action accordingly".

3 Aim for fast and focussed information and feedback.

It is better to ask seven simple questions about a specific activity than to ask thirty questions about everything you do. Build reaction and follow up measures into work practices so that user views and satisfaction can be picked up regularly rather than as an imposed externally driven exercise.

4 Offer choices and options.

One agency found it useful to offer people choices and options to comment on rather than questions like "how can the service be improved"? Asking people to evaluate which of fifteen features of a service were most important to them produced some useful information. Starting out with questions like "what do you need?" generally did not.

5 A lasting dialogue rather than a one off exercise

One idea is to create learning organisations which have been described as organisations that develop the learning of all of their members and are involved in continuously transforming themselves. Listening and learning from the people who use the organisation should not be a one off exercise such as an external evaluation or a consumer survey. We need to build structures and systems that are open to reactions, feedback and new ideas. Managers need to become skilled in and interested in listening, evaluating and finding things out.

6 Evaluate expectations

Sometimes organisations are reluctant to ask users what they want in case it creates unrealistic expectations. If this the case then the purpose of the exercise does need careful explanation. However, in some areas, user feedback does need to be considered with reference to the criteria that users have have employed in their evaluation. One agency was initially pleased by the generally positive feedback it got from carrying out a satisfaction audit of its services. However, when it discussed the findings with a panel of users, comments such as "Well you don't really do what I want, but there is nowhere else to go" and "This place is nicer than some of the appalling places I have had to suffer". It is useful to evaluate the existing provision and to distinguish between people's immediate needs are and their longer term requirements.

7 Views about quality change

Quality is not permanent. As consumers our view about what makes a good computer, car or personal service has probably changed quite rapidly over the past five years as changes in technology, practice, values and circumstances have influenced us. The manager of a walk in day centre for homeless people commented that "five years ago we provided one hot meal every day that was often served cold. We have worked hard to improve things. Now the expectation is that there will always be at least a choice of three hot meals which are always served hot. Standards and expectations rise all of the time". Our idea of quality needs to be continually tested and reviewed. We cannot assume that what was felt important three years ago is still relevant now.

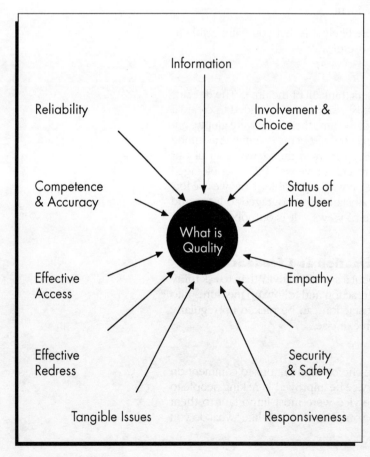

WHAT IS QUALITY?

Trying to reach an exact definition of what makes up quality is difficult.

The following headings are only starting points to help you to identify the quality elements of a particular service. Every service is very different some of the headings may not apply. Some issues may cross over several headings. Under each heading some possible focus areas are suggested. These are not in any sense mandatory. They are only examples.

Information
The availability of information (in different formats) which explains the organisation and the services in a simple way. This could also include access to information, communication systems and how people are kept informed

Examples could include:
- Are all documents written in plain English?
- Is publicity material accurate and up to date?
- Is information available in relevant minority languages?
- Are users kept informed about what is happening?

Reliability
The knowledge that a service will be carried out exactly as agreed and to an agreed time.

Examples could include:
- Are there personal contracts between users and the agency?
- Are appointment times.reasonable?
- Are there contingency arrangements to back up services?

Competence and accuracy.
That the people providing the service have the required degree of skills and knowledge to provide a service in an accurate manner.

Examples could include:
- Are there regular in service training for all staff?
- Do systems exist to check and monitor work?
- Are there relevant professionally qualified staff?

Effective access
That all potential users have an equality of access to services and that the process of contacting the agency for the first time is well managed.

Examples could include:
- Is there effective physical access for people with disabilities?
- Are the agency's services are promoted so that all relevant members of the community can use them?

A common definition of a quality service or product is:

- That it is consistently fit for its stated purpose.
- That it performs to agreed standards.
- That it is responsive to the needs of the user.

How do your organisation's services fit with this definition?

- Are there systems for helping and working with new users?

Effective redress

When things go wrong or when a user feels that they have had poor service or unfair treatment they are able to have things put right quickly.

Examples could include:
- Is there an independent complaints procedures?
- Are there published users rights?
- Are all staff trained to handle informal complaints and criticism in an open and supportive manner?

Tangible issues and appearance

The physical appearance of the service. The effective management of the points of contact between the service and user.

Examples could include:
- Are public areas clean and welcoming?
- Are there effective systems for dealing with callers?
- Are there well managed systems for dealing with telephone callers?

Responsiveness

The ability to provide a service in a personal and thoughtful way.

Examples could include:
- Are there services for clients with specific needs?
- Are there consistent systems for identifying needs?
- Are staff encouraged to respond to diversity?

Security and safety

A freedom from danger, risk or accident. Personal security. Confidentiality.

Examples could include:
- Is there active compliance with health and safety policies?
- Is there protection and management of any potential risk?
- Are there secure systems for managing any confidential information?

Empathy

The degree to which people delivering a service listen to and explain things to an individual user.

Examples could include:
- Are staff trained in communication skills?
- Is there a commitment to involve users?
- Are there systems and processes for encouraging good communication?

Choice and involvement

The ability of a user to influence the type and level of service provided.

Examples could include:
- Are options made available to users?
- Are there processes for users to influence the service?
- Is there active encouragement for feedback?

Status of the user
The dignity of the service user. The degree of respect given to the client.

Examples could include:
- Are there mechanisms for users to participate in decision making?
- How is individual choice encouraged?
- Are there structures for advocacy?

MANAGING A QUALITY PROGRAMME

Four things are needed before starting on a quality programme:

A commitment to quality.
Often managers are evasive about quality. Most management systems are about resource control, output measurement and meeting targets and commitments. It is easy for issues around quality to get lost in the struggle for day to day survival. A genuine commitment throughout to providing services that are responsive to user needs and are of a consistent quality is needed. This has to be demonstrated both by words and action.

A manager of a health project commented that "a lot of our managers were very good at repeating slogans about quality, but did very little about it in practice. The places in the organisation were our quality programme worked was where managers spent time with users, got involved in the detail of resolving problems and encouraged staff to share good practice. They walked the talk."

Sound organisational processes and structures.
The changes involved in implementing a quality programme will test the effectiveness of the organisation's communication and decision making processes. Three things are needed. First there needs to be a clear direction from the top that keeps the momentum going whilst allowing flexibility within a consistent process. Secondly, people will need to share ideas and information in a climate that is positive, constructive and is about learning rather than always finding fault. Thirdly there needs to be clear lines of accountability and responsibility for carrying out tasks to specific deadlines.

Often the process of implementing a quality programme will improve these processes, but some basic structures and ground rules do need to be in place before starting out.

A strategy and structure.
An early decision is to agree what kind of quality initiative to take. Will it be about quality control and quality assurance or more about the ideas of continual improvement in TQM? Will an external framework be used or will you design

and develop your own approach to quality. Everyone involved in the process will need to understand the language and techniques involved and have a sense of why the organisation is taking such steps.

Some resources.

Any new initiative takes up resources. In quality programmes the most demanded resource is often time. Time away from doing the job to evaluate it is often hard to get. Many quality programmes take about twelve to eighteen months to implement. This needs to be thought about and carefully planned. There may be also a financial cost. Bringing up services to standard will usually involve cost. This needs to be recognised and budgeted for.

The quality movement has created many opportunities for consultants to offer their services. External consultants can help in tailoring a process, acting as a catalyst and challenging the ways of the existing order. Be careful that consultants are not placed in the driving seat. If the whole process is managed and implemented by external consultants it is unlikely that much of it will stick. In the language of organisational change - staff will not own it. There is a good chance that the quality initiative will end as soon as the consultant's contract is completed.

MANAGING THE PROCESS

The following seven points are useful in managing the process:

1. Manage it over time

A key responsibility for managers is to make a commitment to see it through. Often in organisations it is easy to be pulled off course and move on to some other "good idea". A quality initiative will take time to develop. There will be times when the initiative does not have much to show for itself as it is still being developed. Sticking to it, preventing it from losing momentum and providing continual guidance is an important management task.

2. Do not take on too much at one time

In many change processes often the hardest thing is to take that first step from discussion to doing. Be careful about taking on far too much and feeling swamped. If too much time is spent on developing the quality system the work will not get done. One organisation developed a rolling programme. It identified sixteen areas in which to develop standards. To keep it manageable it drew up a programme where over a year it worked on four standards at any one time.

3. Build on what you are doing well

A worker in a large national charity complained that "when our managers decided to go for quality the implied message was that what we had been doing previously was not good enough. In fact there was lots of good work going on. It just needed bringing together. Instead we felt written off." Effective quality programmes build on what works now by making it consistent across the organisation. It should be seen as a developmental process building on existing good practice rather than a revolutionary departure from what went on before.

4. Invest in learning

As well as learning about the process of developing quality, people need to be encouraged to learn from each other about what works. They also need to learn from users about their experience and aspirations. Encouraging training, evaluation and more on the job learning opportunities such as secondments, work shadowing and research projects can help to overcome anxiety, assist in the injection of new ideas and give people the confidence to implement the programme.

5. Limit the paperwork

Many quality assurance schemes have suffered from a deluge of paperwork. The emphasis of external schemes such as BS 5750 and Investors in People is in supplying and auditing documentation. One of the worst outcomes is that the quality programme leads to an organisation driven by manuals and formal procedures rather than by responsive and creative individuals. Managers will need to keep a check on written documentation. Training in plain English communication, editing of documents, using an active rather than passive style and limiting the length of documents can all help. In some cases, in particular in standard setting, often the more you write the less clear and specific the standards become.

6. See it as a continual process

Managers need to see the development of quality as a continual exercise rather than a one off process. Clearly there need to be milestones in the process - such as the publication of standards or the award of an external accreditation, but these should not be seen as the end of the exercise. Managers can help by encouraging reviews of existing standards, encouraging people to share ideas and practices and by showing their personal commitment to gradual but continual improvement.

7. Now might not be the right time.

High demands for services, pressures on time and money and an unstable external environment are permanent features of life in many organisations. They mitigate against new initiatives. There is probably never going to be a perfect time to do it, so often managers have to be bold and make the time for an initiative. However, there may be some occasions when it would be unwise to launch a quality initiative. The director of a museum faced with having to implement an organisational restructuring and having to cope with a 5% reduction in funding concluded that "although I am very committed to it, I do not feel that we have either the time or energy to do it properly. Individuals in the staff team are anxious about their own job security. We need to reconsider it in six months time".

A MODEL FOR IDENTIFYING SERVICE QUALITY

One of the hardest tasks in finding out what are the important quality elements in a service is trying to see the organisation as people outside of it may see it. Often the people working in it are too close to it to question how it works or to review its effectiveness. An interesting approach to this was developed by three American academics who studied quality from the point of view of a person using a service rather than that of a person purchasing a product.

IDENTIFYING SERVICE QUALITY

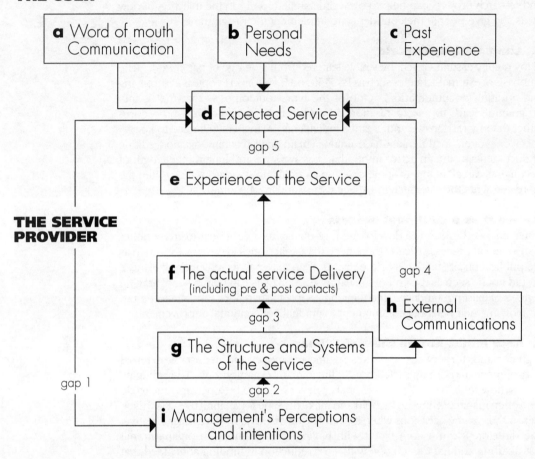

THE USER

a Word of mouth Communication

b Personal Needs

c Past Experience

d Expected Service

gap 5

e Experience of the Service

THE SERVICE PROVIDER

f The actual service Delivery (including pre & post contacts)

gap 3

g The Structure and Systems of the Service

gap 2

h External Communications

gap 4

gap 1

i Management's Perceptions and intentions

Adapted with kind permission from Parasurman, Zeithami and Berry 1995 with permission from the American Marketing Association from the Journal of Marketing Fall 1985 edition.

Parauraman, Zeithaml and Berry's model can be adapted and developed to look at services from the perspective of someone using a service provided by a voluntary group.

The model has the following attractions:
- It deals with what people "perceive". This is important as quality is often a matter of perception.
- It looks at a service from the point of view of the user rather than from that of a service provider or funding body.
- Its focus is on specific gaps in expectation and actual experience of using the service.

Boxes a. b. and c. are the factors that influence what each service user expects the service to be like. None of these factors is in the direct control of the service provider. They represent a series of messages, rumours, perceptions and actual needs that a person picks up with them before they use the service. The level and accuracy of this information obviously varies from user to user.

Box h, the external communications produced by the service provider may also influence the user. The service provider might communicate through publicity material, media and generally by the image of the service.

Boxes a, b, c and h, therefore combine together to create a perception of "expected service" (box d) This might be a series of positive expectations, or it might be a series of negative ones, or it might be a set of expectations that the service provider regards as unrealistic ones (..."the organisation will be able to solve everything...").

Turning to the service provider, the people who design the service and decide how it should be organised have their views of what users need and want (box h). This might be very accurate and well researched or it could be totally out of touch with users needs and expectations. However, this perception is used along with the level of resources that are available, the policies, history and values of the organisation to design and set up a service (box g).

How the service actually works in practice (box f) is made up of three parts: pre-contact (how the user gains access to the service), the service itself and the post service follow up.

Box e represents what the user actually thinks about the quality and value of the service after using it.

There are a number of gaps which can develop:

Gap 1
A gap between the user expectations and needs and what the people who design, fund and direct think the user needs and wants.

People who design and run services usually see the service in a different way from the people who use it. A management committee of a newly established advice centre thought that people would want a service that was friendly and informal. They therefore decided to have an open plan office. It was later established that users would have preferred the privacy of interview rooms.

Often the problem is one of not understanding what exactly the need is. A number of large organisations have established that people are dissatisfied with having to wait for appointments. They have responded by improving the physical appearance of the waiting area (eg painting the waiting room, providing newspapers etc) when what people really wanted was to have an accurate appointment time that was kept to.

In many agencies, service planners and senior managers have their own view of what they think people want, but it is based on out of date information or a misconception of what is needed or wanted.

Gap 2

A gap between how a service management would like the service to be managed and how it actually performs.

Gap 2 is a management problem. It reflects an inability to run the organisation in the way that the service managers would like to. The gap may well be caused by inadequate funding or other constraints. For example, an agency would like to have wheelchair access to all parts of its building, but cost and design factors prevent it from being able to effect the desired improvement.

It may also be that the service management is unable to bring about the changes in working practice or recruit and retain staff of sufficient competence and skill to provide the level of quality that it would prefer.

Gap 3

A gap between how a services management thinks or believes that the service should operate and how it operates in practice.

Just because there are formal quality standards in place, there is no guarantee that the service will always be carried out in the specified way. It may be that individual workers disagree with or do not properly understand or are not able to work in the way that the organisation thinks they should.

For example, as part of an agency's quality assurance programme it decided that there should always be three staff available during the centre's public opening hours. However, due to staff absences, other pressures and staff not regarding it as being particularly important, on at least two to three occasions in a month sessions were under-staffed. The agency's management did not know that its standards were often not being upheld.

It may not always be negative. Often good work is carried out despite management standards and instructions. Staff find ways of breaking or bending the rules to deliver what people want.

Gap 4

A gap between the day to day reality of the organisation and the image that it creates in its external communications and publicity.

The public image of an organisation may well be very different from how it works in practice. This often creates confused expectations.

A large housing organisation decided that as part of its equal opportunities policy and its commitment to improve the quality of access that all of its publicity material would be translated into minority ethnic languages. This created an expectation amongst members of the public who used a minority ethnic language that if they were to contact a housing office there would be someone there who could speak to them in their language - this was rarely ever the case.

Gap 5

A gap between the users' expectations of the service and the service they actually receive.

Gap 5 is the difference between the service that is delivered and what the user had previously expected. It could be that the service is disappointing (.."I expected that the problem could be sorted out quickly...they tell me now that it will take weeks") or that the quality of service exceeds expectations (..."I did not realise that the service was free..").

This model has three distinct advantages:

- It looks at a service from a users point of view - turning the way the service operates inside out.
- It provides staff with a framework to research and establish what exactly are the gaps in how a service is designed and operates.
- It can help an organisation to identify what action it needs to take to reduce the gaps and provide a more responsive service.

CHAPTER FIVE

Quality Control & Quality Assurance

Quality control often conjures up an image of a white coated inspector at the end of a factory assembly line checking if the products made by workers on the line are good enough to be shipped out to customers. Quality control has the following features:

1 It is retrospective. It is about checking what has been done or is being done.

2 It is about ensuring that work conforms to a specification.

3 It involves a separate person or function acting as an inspector or auditor who is external to the people who deliver the service or product.

Examples of quality control might include:
- The manager of an advice centre checking one in ten casework sheets to check the accuracy of advice given.
- A local authority inspector carrying out random inspections on a centre with which it has a contract with to ensure compliance with the terms of the agreement.
- A trainer asking course participants to fill in a course review form at the end of a course to see if the course's design and delivery was appropriate.

Quality control is a necessary part of any management operation or quality process. It happens in most organisations on an organised or random basis.

However, there are serious weaknesses in relying solely on quality control:

It is expensive

The process of doing something, finding out that it has been done incorrectly and then having to put it right is costly and inefficient. In larger organisations the cost of having to have external or internal control functions can be expensive.

It is reactive

Quality control is often about having to "close the stable door after the horse has bolted". It can create an inefficient and dysfunctional system where things are allowed to go wrong and then put right.

It is negative

Quality control systems can create a management style that is all about "catching people out". Managers or inspectors adopt an approach where they learn to focus on what is wrong rather than right, look for faults rather than achievements and are perceived as unconstructive and unhelpful.

It all depends on external control system

By separating out the control system from the process of doing the work problems can occur. Tensions and conflicts occur between people doing the job and those inspecting it. The system depends upon the ability of the external inspector to be up to date with what they are inspecting.

Quality control will always have a role in most organisations

The negative nature of its operation can be at odds with the developmental and creative elements of quality assurance and total quality management. It should only really be seen as one limited element in a quality system.

DEVELOPING QUALITY ASSURANCE

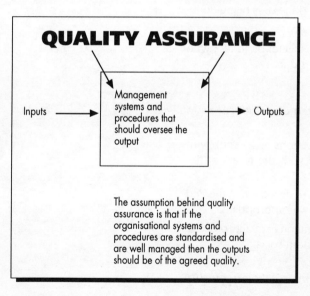

QUALITY ASSURANCE

Inputs → Management systems and procedures that should oversee the output → Outputs

The assumption behind quality assurance is that if the organisational systems and procedures are standardised and are well managed then the outputs should be of the agreed quality.

Quality assurance is based on three things:

- Feedback from users that leads to a clear view on what constitutes the quality elements of a service.

- The setting of standards that underpin the quality factors.

- Management effort to make sure that the standards are consistently met and can be improved.

A standard is not a target or vague policy commitment. The main thrust of quality assurance is that the organisation should be expected to perform consistently to set standards of good practice. The standards act as minimum guarantees that users and purchasers can expect from the organisation.

Quality assurance aims to achieve a consistency of service delivery. It needs to ensure that services perform to an agreed level and removes the element of chance in being a service user. An assistant director of a voluntary agency commented that

"Someone using our services had to expect pot luck. Workers in the same team doing the same job did it entirely differently. Everyone had their own style and approach. The level of resources available to do the job varied from team to team. We left workers to do the job how they thought best. Sometimes the client would get a Rolls Royce service other times a scruffy mini cab. Levels of service varied from excellent to embarrassingly awful. There was no agreement about the minimum expectations about how the job should have been done. We got into quality assurance as a way of achieving an equity amongst users and to clarify our own expectations."

Achieving consistency can be hard. Done badly it can take away flexibility and responsiveness. Or even worse the standards can be set so low that it cements bad practice - " the service is not what is wanted, it does not work and I do not enjoy it, but at least it is consistent...".

For it to work well quality assurance must be informed by what users think is important and also the best achievable practice within the organisation. It should be about sharing and consolidating good practice and making users much more aware of what to expect from a service.

ONE APPROACH TO QUALITY ASSURANCE

The approach suggested here is an outline one with which any organisation would need to develop around it its own processes and structures around.

It is based around five stages:

A clarification stage
The purpose of this stage is to make sure that the organisation has a clear idea of exactly what business it is in, what it thinks is important about how it works and that it has identified who are the intended service users.

DEVELOPING QUALITY ASSURANCE

Clarification
Agreeing the organisation's values.
Establishing what the mission is.
Clarifying who the service users are.

Learning
Finding out what users regard as a "quality" service.
Identifying best practice.

Standard setting
Developing key measurable "quality standards".

Developmental
Identifying gaps between current practice and the quality standards.
Investing in training, systems, and support to ensure that standards can be met.

Launching it
Publishing Quality Assurance Standards

This stage for some organisations might be straightforward. Often, however, they can provoke some lively debate and discussion. Before embarking on the quality assurance the organisation needs to be sure exactly what it is meant to be doing and for whom. Tensions about purpose and values and conflicting expectations between different stakeholders do need resolving at this stage.

A learning stage
There are two elements in this stage; first to find out what users regard as a "quality" service and secondly to identify best practice within the organisation.

69 •

SETTING STANDARDS

One of the first issues in developing quality assurance is to identify the areas for standards. You need to agree a manageable framework that includes all the important activities that matter. Having too many standards makes the process difficult to manage and often leads to an over bureaucratic approach to quality assurance.

One useful technique is to map out the processes and steps that users pass through from their first contact with the organisation through to any end point. This map may need to take into account the different routes into the organisation and also the role of other agencies in referring and passing on users.

Standards also need to be developed for the internal administrative and managerial tasks that are necessary to provide the direct services.

The Washington Counselling Centre

Washington Counselling Centre identified eleven areas for developing standards which were in their view the important stages in the way clients contacted, used and "exited" from the centre. They also identified four areas for standards which reflected essential management and support practice necessary to keep the organisation together.

Project teams drawn from the core staff team, the management group and sessional workers researched clients positive and negative experiences of each area and identified good practice for each area. They then produced a draft standard for each area.

For the four internal management standards, front line staff and the management group were regarded as the users. They were surveyed to find out their views of quality and also their expectations of the management and support systems.

The whole process took over a year with three to five project teams in operation at any one time. Each project team worked to a three month deadline and reported back to a staff meeting. The final drafts were task orientated, measurable and each limited to a half page in length.

The final document was approved by the management group after a final discussion with three groups of current and former clients. The centre's main purchaser, the local health authority, had supported the process and had recognised that the process would take time to do properly.

The centre's management group have decided that each standards document should be be reviewed on a six monthly basis to see if there are any areas where the service is regularly below standard or areas where the standard is proving to be too easy to meet.

IDENTITIFYING AREAS FOR STANDARDS

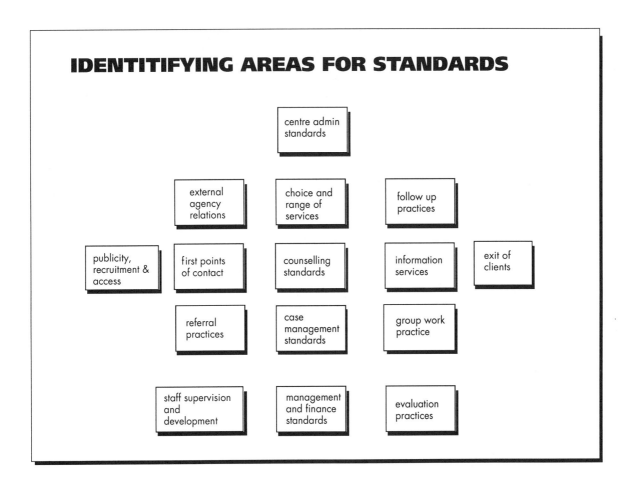

This is possibly the most difficult part of the process. It is the stage that many public and private organisations have avoided and consequently relied upon a belief that they as professionals know best. They simply write standards based on what they are doing already. The objective of the process is not to end with a definitive users view of what is quality. Rather the objective is to create a continual process of learning from users and intelligently use it in designing quality standards.

The second element is to identify existing best practice within the organisation.

It is important to focus on finding what the organisation does well and using that as a basis of good standards. Often managers find this hard as they have developed an antennae which look for what is going wrong rather that what is going right. Good practice is either ignored or taken for granted.

The process of looking for good practice needs to be a participative one. For example, a social care project might find that its clients feel strongly that information that the project might have about client circumstances should be treated confidentially. Identifying best practice is about finding the best way in which user expectation can be met. Often, even in small organisations people do the same job very differently. One worker might make sure that all case papers are locked away, another might have a system for destroying client papers when the case closes. Others might have different approaches. Through team work, discussions and analysis it would be possible to draw out a consistent practice that should meet client needs and provide a more consistent working practice.

Best practice should ideally come from finding out what the organisation does well. It might be useful also to look at how similar organisations approach a problem or task and see if their ideas could be adopted. This practice, common in some industries, is known as "bench marking" and is about establishing a sector wide standard of best practice.

STANDARDS NEED TO BE:

Clear
Specific
Measurable
Attainable

A standard setting stage

This stage is about turning organisational best practices into a limited number of measurable quality standards.

Standards need to be:

Clear.
They need to be written in a language that is active and unambiguous.

Specific.
They need to set out what the user can expect and be as precise as possible.

Measurable.
The organisation needs to be able to know if the standards are not being met or if the standard could be raised.

Attainable.
The organisation must have the resources to meet the standard.

Most organisations do have some sort of standards already in place. It is useful to consider if standards might already exist and can be developed into a quality framework. Possible standards might come from:

Professional ethics and values.
Some professional bodies produce clear professional standards for their members to uphold.

External policy.
Purchasing or funding bodies might make compliance with a standard a contract condition.

National codes of practice.
There may be nationally agreed codes of best practice that you could support. For example, The Commission for Racial Equality produce several good practice guides.

Analysis of past mistakes.
A critical review of past incidents and errors might form the basis of standards.

In considering external sources of standards the following points needs to be considered:
Are they really what users want?
Are they clear and specific enough?

Standards must be written down and documented in an easily accessible way. Experience suggests that this needs careful management. If too much is written down, the standards can become inaccessible or too detailed. There is a worrying tendency to believe that organisations can be managed by procedural manuals alone. The documented standards need to be easy to understand, easy to refer to and written in a task centred and active way.

STANDARDS THAT LOWER PERFORMANCE

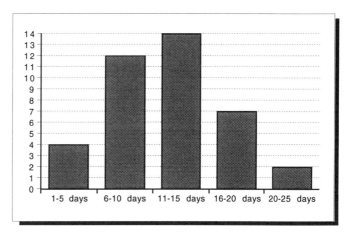

A local authority decided to develop quality standards for various activities. One of the first services to develop a quality standard was an environmental improvement unit. One of the unit's main tasks was to receive, process and approve minor requests for environmental improvements. The unit team leader carried out a quick survey that showed that the time involved in the unit's initial response to applications varied considerably:

- At best the unit was able to complete the process in under five days and at worst it could take anytime up to twenty five days. The team leader could see little real reason for such a range.

- When he came to set standards he was unsure of what an appropriate time should be. Under pressure from his team and to "be on the safe side" he set the minimum standard at eighteen days.

- Three months later performance has averaged out. Most applications are processed at or around eighteen days. Now, no applications are processed under fifteen days.

- A clear case of formal standards reducing effective performance.

- In setting standards there is a difficult balance to get right. The standard must be achievable and realistic. There is no point in setting a standard that cannot be met. On the other hand standards must also be challenging and based on achievable good practice.

- In this case perhaps the team leader should have spent his time finding ways to increase performance before writing a standard.

A developmental stage

After setting the standards, but before launching them, the organisation needs to check that it is capable of meeting the standards. Managers will need to identify gaps between current practice and the intended quality standards and draw up action plans. The organisation will need to be prepared to invest in training, resources and back up systems to ensure that standards can be met.

A launch stage

Quality assurance standards have different implications for different parties

For funders and purchasers they should have the confidence that the service they pay for is operating to consistent standards. Their involvement in reviewing standards and ensuring that standards are monitored will need to be agreed.

The user should have a clearer understanding of what they can expect from a service and what rights they have. Users should benefit from a more responsive service. One organisation edited their quality assurance document into a users guide to the organisation that set out minimum expectations and rights in a punchy and clear format?

The purchaser

POTENTIAL
BENIFITS OF
QUALITY
ASSURANCE

The service provider

The service user

The standards should make it clear to the user what they can and cannot expect from the service. It should set out their rights. The process of setting standards should be a participatory and on going one in which service users are actively involved in determining priorities and needs.

The service provider should have a clear understanding of the minimum requirements and expectations that they have to meet. It should help the provider to manage, budget and train staff to ensure that the service can always meet the standard.

QA should give the purchaser a confidence that the service that they fund or contract for should perform to agreed minimum standards. The purchaser may wish to be involved in making sure that the standards are being met.

A TEMPLATE FOR DOCUMENTING STANDARDS

**What is
the standard?**

**How will it
be monitored?**

**What rights
will users have?**

**How will the
organisation
make sure
that the standard
can be met?**

STANDARDS PLUS - IMPROVING THE STANDARD

An exercise that might develop out of agreeing minimum standards is to identify "standards plus" - levels of service which the organisation would like to be able to meet i.e. is above the threshold of the standard, but cannot always guarantee. For example, an information service might have a quality standard of responding to every enquiry within three working days. If it is able to meet this standard, it could then go on to commit itself to a "standard plus" policy of a two day response time and a three month follow up telephone call to every fifth user to check on the effectiveness of the information provided. It could then monitor itself to see how many times it exceeds the standard. This could indicate that the original standard is too low, or that the staff have reached a level of competence where their performance is excellent.

Standard	Standard Plus	Action Plan
All enquiries answered in 3 days	Target response time 2 days	Improve technology
		Monitor response
	Follow up 1 in 5 enquiries to check on effectiveness of response	Design feedback system
		Find staff time to do follow up work

The organisation may experience benefits of more consistent work practices and more clarity about what is expected of them. Managers in the agency should be able to use the standards as a tool for staff development, supervision and organisational development.

The process does not end with the publication of a quality assurance document. Users and their expectations change. The dialogue with users needs to continue and reflecting change.

Some organisations have developed "standards plus". For example a standard in a residential home might be to provide a choice of two social activities a week. Staff might decide that through their effort and with some extra resource they might be able to deliver three activities. This is not a guarantee, but might help the service to develop.

There is a risk of becoming complacent at the end of the process. Some companies have set standards deliberately low, so that they will easily achieve them. Very soon the standard becomes the norm - no-one ever bothers to work beyond it. One strategy is to build in service improvement plans for each area, setting out how standards will be improved over time.

MANAGING THE PROCESS

The following points need to be considered:

Being consistent and flexible at the same time
There is danger that quality assurance could lead to unresponsiveness and a lack of flexibility. "If it is not in the standard - we don't have to do it". A useful counter balance to this is to see standards as a base structure for the organisation from which staff can respond to the needs of each user. One agency worked hard to ensure their standards stressed opportunities for flexibility, choice and innovation.

Internal and external standards
As well as setting standards for what the external user or consumer of the service should be able to expect, standards also should be set for the internal processes necessary to keep the organisation going. These could include financial information, personnel and training, and management support and supervision. The idea of asking management and support staff to think of what they do as a service to "front line" staff can be a challenging one.

Mixed expectations
There may be occasions when you cannot agree to a standard that users want. It could be that resources are not available. Or it could be that the organisation decides that it is not in the interest of the user to provide it. It could be that your professional view is that it is undesirable or that other constraints such as legal or contractual obligations prevent you from so doing. If this is the case then this needs to be acknowledged and dealt with in an assertive way. It should not be ignored or avoided. One local authority published a set of standards that made it very clear that in policy terms they would like to do more, but were limited by spending constraints. Quality assurance has to be about realistic expectations of what the service can deliver and not about vague policy commitments of how you would like services to be in a perfect world.

BS5750 - AN EXTERNAL STANDARD

Any study of quality management would soon touch on BS5750. In the last few years, helped by intensive marketing and government support, BS5750 has established itself as a benchmark for quality. Its full correct title is BS EN ISO 9000.

BS5750 is a national standard awarded after a process of independent assessment. It sets out the steps and processes suppliers and manufacturers must take in order to be awarded BS5750. It does not prescribe specific standards for an individual product or service, rather it tests the system that produces the product or service.

To register for BS5750 an organisation is required to produce detailed systems, usually in the form of a quality manual, which is reviewed by an external assessor (usually a consultancy company or the British Standards Institute itself).

In response to growing criticism of BS5750 that it is bureaucratic, costly and inappropriate for smaller organisations BSI launched at the end of 1994 a special assessment scheme for small firms who employ between 1 to 10 people. The launch price was £990 for the first assessment and £710 for annual assessment.

BS5750 has made considerable in roads in some parts of the public sector, but less so in the voluntary sector. The Leonard Cheshire Foundation has had accredited three homes and one domiciliary care service as part of a rolling programme to develop a quality assurance system for all of its services.

Advocates of BS5750 argue that it has the following advantages:
It is a statement that the organisation has systems and procedures for producing a product or service. They have been independently inspected and are subject to regular audit.

By referring to BS5750 accreditation it might assist in establishing external credibility in order to win contracts. In some industries holding BS5750 is a prerequisite to applying for contracts or becoming an "approved supplier".

The process of obtaining BS5750 may well improve the organisations internal processes and management. An important argument in quality assurance is "get it right first time" - that doing things properly in the first instance is always cheaper and quicker than making errors and having to put them right later.

Critics of BS5750 point out that its award does not indicate that a service or product is of a particular quality. It is only concerned with the processes and systems involved in planning for, managing and controlling quality. An organisation could obtain BS5750 by setting its standards low and not consulting with its users - all it has to do is gets its procedures in order.

There is some debate about the ease of application of BS5750 to a "people" sector such as social care. BSI do suggest that it can be adapted to any type of organisation.

The total cost of registration could be prohibitive for many organisations. The staff time involved in preparing for assessment is considerable and would need to be budgeted for. There is also a risk of too many systems, procedures and manuals creating an organisation run by a rule book which de-motivates staff and reduces the flexibility of the organisation.

BS EN 9000

The organisation must be able to demonstrate that it has systems and management procedures in place which ensure quality.

The following elements are usually included:

• Quality Assurance Policy	• Statistical systems
• Training in quality for all staff	• Management information
• Clear staff responsibilities for quality	• Organisational procedures
• Inspection and testing systems	• Effective purchasing policies
• Quality control checks	• Systems that will identify errors
• Systems that can "trace" work	• An audit process for quality

EXAMPLES OF STANDARDS
FROM THREE DIFFERENT ORGANISATIONS

Three different organisations; a counselling service, a youth work agency and the finance department of a large housing association used the same format for drawing up standards.

Counselling centre

Standard area:
How first interviews will be carried out.

What is the standard?

At the first interview the counselling process will be explained. Choice of male/female counsellor and appointment times will be offered.

Fees will be agreed and recorded.

Client will be given copy of centre guide.

Youth work agency

Standard area:
The planning of each centre's activity programme.

All young people in membership will be entitled to participate in the programme planning process. Their views must be recorded in centre plans.

Programmes must take into account diversity of interest. The needs of priority groups must be taken into account

All centre managers must have published local systems and structures for user consultation.

Finance department

Standard area:
Production of monthly budget information for line managers.

The monthly budget control report must be with budget holders within 12 days of the month end.

Any agreed errors or changes will be entered within 20 days.

Every budget holder will be assigned to a named central accountant who will meet with the budget holder to review performance at least quarterly.

The report will be in a mutually agreed format.

EXAMPLES OF STANDARDS
FROM THREE DIFFERENT ORGANISATIONS Cont.

How will it be monitored?

Through audit of case records
Through peer reviews
Through 3 monthly client feedback

Through 6 monthly centre evaluation
Though user complaints and
feedback

Through 6 monthly satisfaction
audit
Through internal case audits

What rights will users have?

To have choice over male or female
counsellor and appointment time.
To have process explained.
To have the fee policy explained
and their own fee calculated
in their presence.

To participate in planning meetings.
To meet with the Area Manager
if the programme is unsatisfactory.

To expect reports on time.
To request a change in report format.

How will the organisation make sure that the standard can be met

Through counsellor training.
By providing an interview checklist.
By always allowing 45 minutes for
the first interview.

Through training in user involvement.
By making available user consultation
material.
By Area Managers being available to
assist in programming activities.

Through the provision of agreed
computer time and resources.

CHAPTER SIX

Total Quality Management

Total Quality Management (TQM) is more of a movement of ideas than a set of systems and standards. It builds on much of the work involved in quality assurance but requires a much more in depth and radical look at how the organisational processes and systems create and improve the quality elements of how a service is organised.

The following themes are at the heart of TQM:

1. Identifying supply chains

Supply chains are the sets of internal and external relationships that must work together to meet user needs and aspirations. For a class teacher to teach she will need the classroom cleaned, books and resources provided, the timetable organised so that everyone is in the right place and the availability of professional support and help. The idea behind a supply chain is that there is little point just focusing on the quality of primary activity (the teacher teaching her class) if all the activities that lead up and support it are not coordinated and managed.

2. The idea of internal customers

The aim of a TQM organisation is that everyone has a customer. A finance section could decide that its customers are the departmental managers whose budgets they administer, employees on the payroll and perhaps external suppliers and contacts with whom the organisation has accounts. To provide a service to an internal customer means clarifying and understanding their needs and expectations. Do managers find the reports prepared by the finance section helpful? Would they prefer more frequent reports or reports in a different format?

3. Continual and constant improvement

TQM places great emphasis on problem solving; overcoming the blocks and barriers that get in the way of providing a consistent quality, encouraging innovation and evaluation throughout. Through constant measurement and review (sometimes called "statistical process control") and the use of problem solving teams (sometimes called quality circles) there is a push to improve the effectiveness of the system and the quality of its output. "Aim for constant 1% improvement 100% of the time" is one of the many slogans of advocates on TQM.

4. Team work and co-operation

TQM often requires a "cultural revolution" in how an organisation manages its operation and employs people. Often the invisible barriers that exist in an organisation have to be challenged. One housing association found that many problems experienced by tenants were caused because each department involved only looked at it from their departmental or professional perspective. Many problems could be a housing management issue, a maintenance issue and a financial issue all at the same time, yet tenants problems were often lost in the systems or only partly dealt with. TQM demands that the whole picture is seen, that people and systems work together and that the organisation be designed (or "re-engineered") to ensure a unity of purpose and a holistic approach.

FEATURES OF TOTAL QUALITY MANAGEMENT

Constant Improvement.

A user centred approach.

Measurement and feedback throughout.

Preventative action

---

5. Prevention rather than crisis management

TQM places great emphasis on "getting it right first time". It challenges the negative emphasis of quality control by stressing the importance of staff development, empowering people to respond to problems quickly and encouraging innovation. Organisations need to have reward, communication and management systems that encourage quality work and constant improvement.

The way in which TQM is sold by management gurus and the quality industry can be off putting. Sometimes people can be irritated by the sloganising of its supporters. There is also a danger of being convinced that it is a panacea that can be applied to any organisation regardless of its complexity and purpose.

Perhaps the most useful element of TQM is the recognition of the need for radical internal change in how an organisation works and manages.   Often quality programmes do not get beyond the "charm school approach" of customer care. One individual described her organisation's experience of a quality programme as:

"Our directors were sold the idea of quality at a conference. They came back and started using new words that nobody else seemed to understand. They went overboard about packaging the service - one stop shops, training staff in customer care and telephone skills with a new logo and a lick of paint in the reception. All good ideas on their own. The problem is that much of the core service is badly designed, badly managed and badly delivered. All of this new packaging merely provides a temporary camouflage".

One of the main gurus in quality, W. Edwards Deming, stresses that one of the key issues is getting the system right throughout. He talks of how in most organisations managers identify problems as being problems with people. They want to find better ways of organising, managing or controlling staff. His observations suggest that often problems are rooted in a system or structural issue rather than a people problem Change the existing people with new people and sooner or later the original problems will return.

The changes needed in the stucture of an organisation are often illustrated by drawing the traditional organisation as a triangle:

At the top of the triangle are senior managers who make policy and set the direction. In the middle are managers and supervisors who transmit the policy and direction and control resources. At the bottom of the triangle are the people who do the work and deliver the service to the user.

In many organisations, the implicit message is that the more contact you have with the user the less rewards you get and the less status you have. Most career structures are designed so that you do more direct work early on in your working life and are then promoted away from the user. Pay scales are usually such that the people who have most contact with the user gets paid the least.

The organisation is designed for vertical command and control. New ideas and directions should come from the top and are transmitted to levels below. However, very often the people at the top have little knowledge of what happens at the direct point of contact. What information they have is out of date or has been filtered or edited by the levels below. It assumes that having good ideas is only the concern of those employed at the top of the organisation.

It can become top heavy. Several organisations have very well resourced headquarters staffed with well paid middle managers who see their role as to police and control the level below them. There is often an difference at the service delivery level. Here the service may be at breaking point, understaffed and under resourced struggling to provide a service despite the unremitting torrent of directions and paperwork coming down from above. It is as if what is valued in the organisation is what happens at the centre rather than the core service to the user.

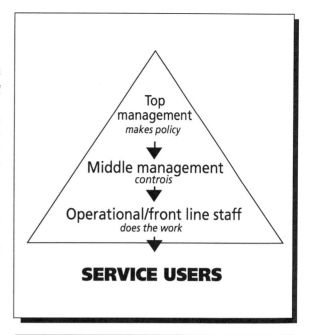

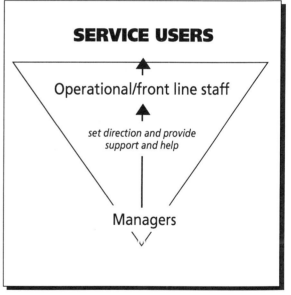

A more radical way to look at the organisation is to draw it as if the user were at the top and people either worked to the user or supported those who were providing the core service.

An organisation designed around this idea would have the following features:

- It would reward, support and focus on the core activity. All other activities and processes would stem from the core activity and be geared at supporting it.

- Although managers would have to retain a direction setting role and a limited control function their main emphasis should be on coaching and supporting staff who in turn deliver the service.

- The role of central functions such as personnel and finance would change. The emphasis of their role would shift from controlling resources and policies to supporting and enabling the staff providing the direct service.

- The organisation would do away with blocks and barriers that prevent fast communication, teamwork across the organisation and feedback. There would be fewer levels of management control but active encouragement for staff involved in the core activity to identify and develop innovative improvements and new ideas.

A TQM analysis of this case would suggest the following:
There are some examples of duplication in this case. Having to complete the registration forms twice and two ambulance trips could probably eliminated through better co-ordination.

Diagnoses could have happened earlier. The ambulance crew and the A&E sister were both sufficiently trained to recognise that the patient would need an X-ray and would need to go to the Orthopaedic ward. Professional boundaries (only the doctor could diagnose) and standing instructions (all ambulances cases must go to the A&E ward) may have got in the way of efficient and effective work. Could the service be designed in such a way as to eliminate the need to visit the A&E ward altogether?

Could technology aid the process? Most days the clerk spent considerable time phoning round for beds - could an open computer system have made this easier? Could there be better links between the ambulance and hospitals? Could only one registration system be necessary?

Could the whole case have been prevented? Would an alarm system have summoned help earlier? The accident was caused by a slip on a worn out carpet. Could something as simple as paying for basic household safety repairs have prevented a costly and distressing emergency?

Only the patient saw the whole issue through. Each step was managed by someone else. The ambulance crew, sister, doctor, clerk and orthopaedic staff all reported to different people and were part of different systems. The ambulance crew were part of an emergency system. The clerk was part of an administrative system. No one managed or even monitored the whole process. In each stage staff worked very hard, but the delays and anxiety involved were caused when the patient was passed from stage to stage.

In carrying TQM exercises the following four issues are often highlighted:
Many organisations are designed around departmental or professional boundaries rather than to create teamwork. Even quite small organisations have "territorial battles" over who is responsible and who is in charge. Often the user is lost in a grey area between the provinces of two specialisms or departments within the same organisation. Could organisations be better designed? Could jobs be better

designed to enable people to see something through from beginning to end? Are multi-skills jobs better than jobs with narrow boundaries? Could people doing the job be given greater power to make decisions and exercise their skills?

There is a lack of information about how things work. The exercise of simply drawing the processes involved in a simple task can be very educative. One grant awarding agency found that to make a simple financial change such as agreeing to move money in one budget to another involved seven different people and could take up to four weeks. In several cases the amount of money involved was significantly less than the cost of the transaction. Getting useful performance measures, listening to feedback from staff and users and carrying out detailed analysis of what really happens are critical starting points in improving quality.

Most organisations are designed for vertical command and control of resources from the top down. Few are actively designed around how people want to use them. One new idea in management thinking has the somewhat awkward title of "Business Process Re-engineering". The essential idea is to see an organisation as a collection of processes. To fulfil a customer expectation the processes need to involve different people and resources. Advocates of re-engineering argue that modern organisations need to be designed around teamwork, flexibility, information and a clear focus on what is important.

It is generally cheaper to invest resources in preventing things from going wrong than in continual crisis management or fire fighting. This often means a quantum leap in management style and behaviour. Managers must shift from seeing their role as a controller to stop things going wrong to a one which is focused on continual improvement and development.

AN EXAMPLE OF A TQM APPROACH

One of the most powerful tools in TQM is to analyse the processes involved in delivering a service and see how the whole process and each component part could be improved.

This case study is an example of such an approach. A hospital doctor observed the systems at work in responding to and processing a simple household accident involving an elderly person. The first step is to set out all of the things that happen and record the different role of each individual or unit. The second step is to analyse it from the following perspectives:

- Did it work?
- Could it be organised better?
- From the user's point of view how could it be improved?
- Is it focused on proactive or preventative action or on reactive crisis management.

The case

1   An old person living alone slips on her kitchen carpet. She is unable to summon help. After three hours the postman and neighbour raise the alarm and phone for an ambulance.

2   The emergency ambulance arrives. The crew provides immediate first aid. They then take the patient to the Accident and Emergency (A&E) ward at the main hospital. It is a standing instruction that all ambulance cases are taken to the A&E ward.

3   On arrival at the A&E ward patient registration forms are completed. An A&E sister conducts a preliminary check to determine priority. The patient will need treatment, but is not an urgent case.

4   After a delay the patient is seen by an A&E doctor who decides that an X-ray will be needed to determine the extent of the fracture. Given her age and that she lives alone she will need an overnight stay in hospital.

5   The A&E clerk has to phone the orthopaedic ward in the neighbouring hospital to arrange a bed. The clerk also has to arrange an ambulance to transport the patient. This takes time.

6   An ambulance transports the patient to the orthopaedic ward in the neighbouring hospital.

7   The patient is then admitted, registration forms filled in and treatment can now commence.

   The whole process took seven hours.

CHAPTER SEVEN

Making Sense Of It All

Several policy makers and managers have become over enthusiastic about measurement and standard setting. They believe that these systems give them accurate levers to control, reward and judge the organisations that they oversee. They continually ask for more information in their search for "objective" evidence. There is a danger that the amount of time involved in collecting information gets in the way of doing the job. There is also a danger of being too scientific about organisational performance. Management is much more of an art than a science. Trying to run an organisation purely by performance measures and indicators will not work. No formal system can take away the need to learn and interpret the context, culture and relationships involved in what you are evaluating. Weather forecast and temperature indicators might become more and more accurate, but we still are inclined to look outside to see if it is raining before we venture out.

This final chapter looks at three issues:
- How the internal and external monitoring process can be improved.
- How measurement and quality issues can become a positive benefit within an organisation.
- How the role of funders and purchasers needs to develop.

IMPROVING INTERNAL AND EXTERNAL MONITORING

Designing performance measurement and quality standards is easiest when the organisation produces a service that is tangible and clear. In such instances it is possible to identify units of activity, service outputs and measures of success. The systems described in this book do require careful application if the activity of the organisation is not particularly tangible or clear cut. The difficulties of determining effective measures can be exaggerated. However, as the Audit Commission said, "the art in performance monitoring lies in ensuring that the measurable does not drive out the immeasurable".

Managers would be foolish to ignore things like teamwork, humour, working styles and informal reactions from users. Review sessions, evaluation workshops, independent appraisals and user meetings may all be needed to give a flavour to the data and information generated through formal measurement.

Some organisations have experienced difficulties in identifying effective systems for campaigning work, creative work and innovative pilots projects and where the aim is to involve the user as much as "service" the user. In these areas measurement and standard setting is possible but special attention needs to be paid to ensure that the reason why is clear, that objectives are sufficiently focused and that the key players have a clear idea of what is good practice.

Measurement of activity, outcomes and quality needs to become an integral part of good management practice. Very often the reasons why something is hard to measure is that its objectives and purpose are not clear. If you cannot measure something, how can you train, manage, support someone else in it? If measurement feels impossible how will you know that you have achieved anything of value?

Be careful about falling into a trap of "watching the scoreboard and not the game." The introduction of a performance measurement system and the attention paid to it could mean that managers focus their attention on getting a "good result on the indicator" and not ignore the informal aspects of the service (atmosphere, staff/ client relations) on which the indicators are unlikely to report on.

A criticism that can be levelled at some funders and purchasers (and some service providers) is that they fail to take the longer term view. Priorities change continually, programmes are expected to deliver results instantly and resource commitments are only made for the short term. One senior manager in a health authority described this situation:

"We have been through countless reorganisations and seem to get a new policy direction by every post. I know that to make real progress in changing people's behaviours will take sustained investment over time. However, the pressure is on me to produce evidence that we are doing something different all the time. New projects are far more interesting to the powers that be than ones which are about long term change".

This pressure can create a monitoring system that is only interested in quick results rather than long term sustainable change. To create real difference usually requires a commitment to the project and an investment of resources longer than one financial year or an annual monitoring cycle. Too much emphasis on the short term can produce quick "flash in the pan results". The former manager of a business development agency commented that ;

"We were brilliant at getting people to set themselves up in their own business. In every monitoring report we would show an increase in new businesses created with our help. Our funders were always very impressed and even held us up as a centre of excellence. I knew from personal contacts that many of the businesses never lasted more than a year. They collapsed very quickly. When we suggested evaluating what happened to a sample of our clients two to three years on we were gently but firmly discouraged. I assume that for political reasons our funder had no interest in a longer term view".

Over a period of time funders policy makers and purchasers need to become more strategic. They need to play more of a part in identifying needs, agreeing objectives and looking for evidence of sound quality work, effective impacts and sustainable outcomes. This may mean doing less day to day monitoring of how the agency operates and more evaluation of medium to longer term results.

In an ideal world, all parties would be able to agree systems which satisfy the funders' need to know that their money is being used properly and the service provider's needs to know how effectively it is meeting its aims, policies and values.

There are occasions when this ideal state can be reached. However, there are times when a funder insists on using indicators which often fail to report anything of value. Sometimes the funder is not interested in establishing useful measures or does not share the same values and policies as the organisation.

If an organisation agrees to use measures that it feels are inappropriate then there is a danger of the measures distorting the internal management process and after a time (in the absence of any other information) setting the direction for the organisation. It may well be that an organisation has to run a performance measurement system to provide "inappropriate" information to a funder and at the same time develop its own internal systems to measure and evaluate the factors that it regards as important.

MEASUREMENT AND QUALITY AS A POSITIVE BENEFIT WITHIN THE ORGANISATION

Monitoring is often met with a defensive and anxious response within an organisation. Staff believe that information is being collected to gather evidence on their personal competence that could be used for negative or punitive motives. In some cases systems have been rigged or tampered with to get a good score.

Careful thought needs to be given as to how to make the process a useful one. The frameworks suggested in this book are all about organisational performance and results and are not directly concerned with the effort and behaviour of individual staff. Clearly the two are linked, but they are different. Individual performance should be dealt with in supervision, appraisals and in general management. Organisational performance and quality is the responsibility of the managers and directors who decide budgets and resource levels and set objectives.

These systems work best when the people who do the job are directly involved in designing the system, carrying out the monitoring and interpreting the results. They need to be built on good practice and should not be seen as an imposition from outside.

Using the information internally
All internal monitoring systems must be linked into plans and activity. In larger organisations it is possible to divide up different levels of information needs. All staff need to know if the organisation is meeting its objectives. They also

Sustainability and long term goals

Direction and objectives

Operational issues

need to get detailed feedback on what is working and what is not working in their particular area. Policy makers, management committee members and trustees need to focus on the longer term strategic issues facing the organisation and to have early warning systems available to inform them if any operational area is failing to meet objectives.

In their book, 'Measure Up', Lynch and Cross developed a pyramid of reporting systems. This was based on a model for private companies, and identified three levels of internal monitoring.

The level one issues were concerned with the longer term viability and purpose of the organisation. They represented a balance sheet of how the organisation was developing. Several key questions need asking at this level:

- Are we viable and are we sustainable?
- How are performing financially?
- Do we have sufficient resources to meet our goals now?
- Are our future plans still viable and sustainable?
- Are we making progress towards our goals?
- Do our activities fit with our client needs, our aims and our values?
- Are we achieving our three year plan?

Level one information was discussed at staff conferences, management team meetings and quarterly trustee meetings. Some of the information was a summary report of level two and three information. Other information came from a rolling programme of evaluation to identify new needs and outcomes. This information was looked at quarterly and formed a crucial element of the strategic planning process.

Level two information was the main concern of the agency's management team made up of the Director and four team leaders. Information at this level was chiefly about medium term strategy and organisation wide issues.

Questions for this level were:
- Are we achieving the results we want?
- Are we implementing the objectives set out in this year's business plan?
- Are there any causes for concern, blocks or barriers that need attention?
- What new opportunities and potential threats need attention.

The management team looked at these issues every month. The information was based on team reports and budget reports placed in the context of the business plan which had very clear and measurable objectives. This information helped the team to provide a "collective steer" to the organisation's work.

Each team had its own level three information reports. They were all concerned and purchasers

One of the biggest changes in the public sector in the past few years has been the development of what has been described as a contract culture. Voluntary organisations have had grant aid contributions converted to service agreement and many now bid for contracts. Compulsory tendering affects many areas of national and local government provision. Many public bodies have been slimmed down to create a small centre that commissions and manages services delivered by others.

This new culture demands a new series of relationships between purchasers and providers. It usually requires a more "arm's length management", where a written agreement sets out mutual expectations and itemises measures and standards which will provide the basis of the monitoring process. However in practice the relationship is often confused. In particular, several voluntary organisations have experienced contradictory and ambiguous relationships with purchasers. A co-ordinator of a local environmental improvement project described it as:

"We are suffering from over monitoring! Our service agreement with the local authority stipulates the monthly reports that we must provide. They run to several pages and take at least a day a month to produce. We also have quarterly review and monitoring visits. So far I cannot think of any single piece of feedback that we have had back from these reports and meetings. We also suffer from the council still treating us as if we are getting a grant rather than carrying out work to a contract. Councillors still want to sit on our management committee (despite a potential conflict of interest) and officers expect to be consulted about internal management issues such as changes in job descriptions."

This diagram suggest the different kinds of relationships that can be developed:

Box 1 Active involvement in the management process.	**Box 4** "Partnership" Regular liaison as well as a formal measurement.
Box 2 Occasional contact through periodic reviews and visits	**Box 3** Arm's length formal contract management.

HIGH

high to low level of contact

LOW ——— *unspecified to specified arrangement* ——▷ HIGH

Active involvement in the management process. (Box 1)

The funding body is significantly involved in the operational management of the voluntary group. It will take a full part in the management process through formal channels (through being very involved in the recruitment and selection of staff) and through regular consultation and full access to management information. This can either be done in a co-operative (or cosy) way or through the funder exercising (or threatening to exercise) a veto.

It could be argued that the voluntary organisation is really only acting as the "agent" of the funder - carrying out their policies and meeting their objectives. The closeness of the relationship can cause some difficulties. For example in negotiating future grants or contracts, the funder would probably have full access to detailed costings which could give them an unfair advantage.

Sometimes problems may occur because the relationship is too unstructured and too informal.

Occasional contact through periodic reviews and visits (Box 2)

The relationship between the voluntary organisation and the funder is not a particularly structured one. It might include the annual production of statistics and a report of work; the authority might expect to attend management committee meetings or carry out infrequent evaluation exercises or monitoring visits. The only real monitoring takes place when the funding arrangement or contract is up for renewal. The funder, working on the basis of "out of sight - out of mind", may find it easier to make cuts.

This type of relationship may give the voluntary group considerable independence to get on with its work as it sees best. However, there is a danger that, because of a lack of communication, the funding body fails to understand or appreciates the group's work and may well carry out a monitoring exercise or make decisions based on ignorance.

Arms length formal contract management. (Box 3)

The relationship that the statutory authority has with the voluntary organisation is the same as it has with all of its other service suppliers (eg. British Telecom). It has formal specifications for the quantity and quality of the service to be provided and at what cost.

The contract (either through its original specification or in an appendix to it) will clearly state the respective responsibilities of the the funder and the voluntary organisation. The contract management process is a carefully structured one between two clearly independent parties.

The relationship is a formal and distant one. How the voluntary agency manages itself is of little concern to the funder provided it provides the service that it said that it would.

Partnership - regular liaison as well as a formal measurement process. (Box 4)

There is some recognition that the voluntary organisation is an independent organisation with its own aims and objectives. Representatives of the funding body are in close contact with the organisation through liaison visits and regular joint meetings.

The relationship is one of providing advice, consultation and planning. It is important that the respective roles are clarified and recorded. There is a potential for the funding body to have "two bites at the cake" - through informal contact (attending management committees) and through a formal contract or performance measurement system.

In reviewing this relationship a number of points are worth considering:

Consistency

In the move from grant aid to a more clearly defined contractual relationship it is important to discuss openly what sort of relationship there needs to be between the parties involved.

One voluntary agency reported negotiating an agreement for providing a service rather than applying for grant. Although there were definite advantages in having a service agreement, it involved the agency in many more management tasks and because of the more explicit nature of the agreement led to a more formal monitoring process by council officers.

The agency's co-ordinator described the new relationship as "the worst of both worlds" in that at one level the council wanted a new, more independent, contractual relationship and at another, councillors wanted to continue to attend the agency's management committee and be fully involved in the management process (including discussions on the negotiating strategy for future meetings with council officers on the funding agreement). In effect, the council had both a formal "arms length agreement" and full participation in the the agency's management process at the same time.

Disparity between different funders

A voluntary group that receives funding or has contracts with more than one source will have to establish a different type of relationship with each funder. Producing different information for different needs, responding to each separate monitoring process and conducting different sets of information will all have implications for staff time and cost.

In developing a strategy for monitoring the following five points are useful for purchasers and funders to consider:

1 What must we know about to satisfy our public duty?

2 What information is needed to check that the service is effective and of appropriate quality?

3 How can we check that the information is being collected accurately?

4 How will we review the information collected?

5 How will we use it to plan and develop?

The relationship changes over time

It is useful to see the relationship as a dynamic one which changes over time. If a group has too close a relationship to its funders then its independence and ability to properly manage itself may suffer. Alternatively, a relationship which is too formal and structured may be inflexible and make negotiating change difficult.

Often change in the relationship is caused by a change in personnel - different people (either on the funders or on the voluntary groups side) may have different perceptions and background knowledge. Or it could be that when adequate funds are available and there is support for the group's work the relationship is more likely to be a close one and when funds are short it is more likely to become distant.

CHAPTER EIGHT

Background Reading

"Outcome Funding" .   £7.95
by Harold S. Williams and Arthur Y. Webb.
Distributed in the UK by NCVO.
Regent's Wharf, 8 All Saints Road, London N1 9RL.
A new approach to public sector grant making.

"Evaluation in the Voluntary Sector".
by Mog Ball
Useful guide to evaluation.

"Working Effectively".   £4.95
By Warren Feek.
NCVO,
Regent's Wharf, 8 All Saints Road, London N1 9RL.
 Step by step approach to self evaluation.

"Performance Measurement - getting the concepts right".
Public Finance Foundation. 1988.
3 Robert Street, London, WC2N 6BH.
Mainly aimed at public sector organisations, a useful guide to core concepts.

"How to lie with Statistics"
Darren Huff.   Penguin Books

"Measure Up"
Richard L Lynch & Kevin F Cross
Mandarin Business Books.
An interesting review of performance measurement in private companies.

"Measuring Quality: The Patient's View Of Day Surgery".
The Audit Commission. May 1991.
1 Vincent Square, London SW1 2PN
Includes an interesting draft questionnaire to find out patient re-action.

"Getting Value For Money."
CIPFA. 1987.
3 Robert Street, London, WC2N 6BH.
The accompanying guide to a video based training pack.

"Value For Money Auditing."
Price Waterhouse.
1990.Gee & Co, South Quay Plaza, 183 Marsh Wall, London E14 9FS.
Detailed guide for Local Authority staff on carrying out value for money
reviews.

"Committed to Quality"
Department of Health, HMSO. 1992
Quality assurance in social services departments

"Purchase of Service"   £9.50
Social Services Inspectorate, HMSO. 1991.
A practice guide to contracting and quality.

"The Search for Quality"
John Stewart and Kieron Walsh. 1989.
Local Government Management Board
Arndale House, Arndale Centre, Luton, LU1 2TS.
Aimed at local authorities, a thoughtful introduction
on quality in service organisations.

"Quality and Contracts".
Association of Metropolitan Authorities. 1991.
35 Great Smith Street, London, SW1P 3BJ.
Case material and practice notes on developing quality assurance.

"Inspecting for Quality"
Social Services Inspectorate, HMSO. 1991.
Guidance to local authorities on the operation of inspection units.

"Guidance document on BS5750 in Social Care Agencies".
The British Quality Association .
10 Grosvenor Gardens, London SW1W 0DQ.

Quality Assurance in the Voluntary Sector.
Rowan Astbury. NCVO. 1993. £5.
Regent's Wharf, 8 All Saints Road, London N1 9RL.

A discussion document on quality.
The Department of Trade and Industry publishes a number of free booklets on
quality management. Although aimed at manufacturing industries, they provide
useful background reading. The publications list is available from the DTI Admail
528 London SW1 8YT Tel. 0171 510 0174
Information regarding BS5750 can be obtained from BSI Quality Assurance,
PO Box 375, Milton Keynes, MK14 6LL.

Measuring and Measuring for Quality
Alan Lawrie. 1995. £35.
Directory of Social Change and NCVO.
24 Stephenson Way, London NW1 2DP
Training pack.